THE BEST OF "MARKETING"

Volume I

Products and Policies

The Best of
"Marketing"

Volume I

Products and Policies

Editor
Michael Rines

LEVIATHAN HOUSE
LONDON

FIRST PUBLISHED IN VOLUME FORM 1975

© Leviathan House Ltd. 1975

Contents originally published in article form in
various issues of *Marketing* Magazine

ISBN for Series   0 900537 30 2

ISBN for Volume 1   0 900537 31 0

ISBN Paperback   0 900537 361

Printed in Great Britain by
Billing & Sons Limited, Guildford and London

CONTENTS

FOREWORD

by

PETER B. BLOOD, F. Inst. M.,
Director General, Institute of Marketing

I am delighted to have been asked to write the foreword to this new book. First, because I find the title – *The Best of Marketing* – splendidly evocative and entirely appropriate to the articles which follow. Secondly, because I have always thought it desirable that many of the excellent practical contributions appearing in the Institute's monthly journal should have a longer life and wider circulation. I congratulate the publishers of these volumes, Leviathan House, on their initiative and perception.

This first volume deals with Policies and Products (I hope the publishers will not object to me reversing the sequence!) and it is in the field of establishing marketing policy where I am sure so many companies have failed. Lip service is paid to a belief in the marketing concept but little else stems from this apart, perhaps, from changing the title on the sales manager's door. If we may define marketing as the management process responsible for identifying, anticipating and satisfying customer requirements profitably, then it is apparent that the customer must become the focal point of the company's entire commercial activity. I submit, therefore, that a genuine understanding and acceptance of the marketing concept means that we must inevitably redefine the first and essential purpose of our business as being to secure and to keep customers. By redefining and restating the priority function of the business in this way, a totally different and far more rewarding philosophy of customer service will permeate throughout the organisation. The potential influence of this outlook at shop floor level is highly significant since for years the workers have been told that the chief purpose of the business is to make a profit. Profit for whom? But let it not be thought that I am suggesting profit is not vital to any enterprise. It most certainly is, but I believe that its achievement is one of the requirements of the business and not its primary function. The relative importance of customers and profit can be illustrated by the fact that it is perfectly possible – however undesirable – to run a business for a time without making a profit. It is not possible to continue the business for one day without customers.

This outlook towards the importance of customers does nothing other than to restate, in terms of policy and action, the basic marketing concept. Nevertheless, these remarks do reflect the change through which marketing is now passing. The pressures of consumerism, the so-called affluent society, the problems of product complexity and increasing customer awareness are all indicating a subtle change in the marketing concept. The philosophy of attempting to satisfy customer "desires" is now altering towards an attempt to satisfy, more particularly, the customer's long-term interests. There are increasing criticisms that "marketing" has merely stimulated short-term trivial wants and has left the customer spiritually denuded in a materialistic desert. I cannot accept this viewpoint, but I do believe that marketing men must increasingly realize that they are, inevitably, an important part of our social fabric and that, as such, they cannot escape their appropriate share of social responsibility. So that if marketing policies are changing, so must the products. Better utilization of expensive, scarce raw materials suggests the return to higher quality goods. More products must be designed with a second use in view and there seems little doubt that packaging must undergo a radical change, not only to meet circumstances of economic recession, but to accord with a changing social philosophy.

So it is that now, more than ever before, the marketing man will need to be better educated in his profession as well as being more alert to the social environment and its increasing effect upon company policies.

ABOUT THE EDITOR

Michael Rines, the 41-year-old Editor of *Marketing*, became a professional journalist in 1970 after 13 years in industry.

He took a law degree at Oxford and then became a sales trainee with a non-ferrous tube manufacturer. One of his first jobs was to handle customers' complaints. His next role was in production management where he acted as the department's link with the sales departments. This was followed by a sales management job in which he had experience of the full range of marketing activities, including the development and launching of new products. From here he became an internal consultant and was involved in the introduction of a management by objectives scheme. Work on organization restructuring, particularly in the marketing area followed.

Rines' first journalistic effort was a series of satirical articles about management subjects which were printed in *Management Today*. These were written while he was still in industry and centred round a fictitious company, but they were so true to life that many readers were surprisingly angry when they realized they had been had.

As a result of the success of these articles Rines was appointed Editor of *Marketing*. Since then he has written regularly for the *Financial Times* and other papers and broadcast on management subjects.

As befits a Yorkshireman, he used to play a lot of cricket and has the unique distinction of having acted as twelfth man for the Australians on an occasion when they were beset by injuries.

ABOUT "MARKETING"

Marketing is the monthly journal of the Institute of Marketing, and has been published since the early twenties. The Institute itself was founded as long ago as 1911 and today it has 16,000 members, and another 16,000 student members are currently studying for the degree standard Diploma in Marketing.

For the past seven years, *Marketing* has been published for the Institute by Haymarket Publishing Ltd., who also publish *Management Today*, *Accountancy Age*, *Campaign* and *Computing*.

Marketing is the only UK magazine covering the whole field of marketing, right through from market research to advertising, selling and distribution. Because it has to cover such a wide range of subjects, it could not attempt to deal with any single one in great depth. Instead, it has concentrated on providing practical advice on dealing with topical issues that affect marketing men.

Its articles, by some of the country's foremost practitioners, are written in simple, jargon-free language.

WHEN AND HOW TO BUY MARKET RESEARCH

"The first awareness of the need for research can be a dramatic moment of truth," writes Mary Griffin, MBE.

To be a spectator at the tribal dances performed when research consultants engage in buying each other's services is to observe in the last movements an attempt to extract blood from stones. This, by the natural laws, is doomed to end in less than satisfaction, but the exercise has much to teach the layman essaying that seemingly uncharted jungle where he must go to buy marketing research services.

When professional treats with professional, the buyer is precise as to his needs, certain about the purpose of the research, definite about the intended end uses, and acutely conscious of the cost benefits which must ensue before it can be wholly justified. Because in this situation the buyer is himself skilled in research, he is realistic about the limits of achievability, and is purchasing for ultimate resale.

The frictions at this interface illustrate the fact that bargains are rarely available when buying research and that many of the apparent choices hold dangers for the unwary. Some firms seeking to lessen uncertainty are alert to these dangers and have sought refuge by acquiring services they can control and monitor closely, but many more are hesitant about the relative merits of in-company resources and consultancy/agency services, or on how to mix the two.

For the purpose of this article it is assumed that the decision to carry out market research is well founded. Nevertheless, examination of the reasons for carrying out the research will help not only in deciding whether to undertake the project as an in-company project but also in choosing among several agencies should a decision be made to go outside.

It is particularly important to stop to establish the reasons for the research when, as is too often the case, the need for it arises from some crisis. At such times, the urge for action is paramount and the signals, which in themselves may indicate the correct decision, may go unnoticed.

The wisest counsel then is to stop, do nothing and think: think why is research needed, what information is required and how it will help when it has been obtained. In this way it is possible to ensure that the problem is correctly analysed and interpreted, and is judged in the context of total operations. Only then can a rational decision be made either to use an existing in-company unit, to set one up if it does not already exist, or to go to an outside agency for help on either a permanent or temporary basis. There are a number of considerations, both internal to the company and external to it, which must be taken into account in making the decision.

Internal considerations

There are business operations where formal research requirements are spasmodic and spaced at long intervals. Here an internal researcher may tend to be under-employed, and a firm whose research requirements are essentially of this kind is likely to be better served, and to achieve greater cost effectiveness, by reliance on agency or consultancy services. The probable continuity of research demand is, therefore, the first determinant of whether an in-company research facility should be developed.

The first awareness of a need for research can be a dramatic moment of truth. This dawning may highlight the fact that not only is research needed on a continuing basis now, but also that it has been an unrecognized need for a long time past. Even then it is not imperative that an internal capability be established: it is not only feasible, but sometimes economically and technically preferable for a firm to rely wholly on external services. Nevertheless, when the demand for research emerges as likely to continue, one member of staff must be charged with the overall task of monitoring and interpreting research needs and information flow. For a while, this function may be carried out by a member of the management team, and a separate research appointment will be necessary only when the task becomes burdensome. Some firms prosper happily and with maximum cost effectiveness without in-company research resources and enjoy good working relationships with the agencies on which they rely: there is no insuperable rule of business which states that each and every firm must at a minimum employ one researcher.

In many cases, of course, the crisis which confirms the need for research will not await the engagement of the required staff. Appreciable time may pass before an appointment could be made, and even after the appointment there must nearly always be a period of indoctrination before an internal researcher can act effectively. In such cases there must be initial reliance on contract research, but the internal researcher should be hired as early as possible during the course of the commissioned project and given the opportunity of working alongside the agency in monitoring the research programme. He should subsequently carry out, as his first major responsibility, dissemination of the research findings within the firm. Frequently this proves to be a happy way of introducing research within a company, and of ensuring that it becomes one of the routine tools of management.

The alternatives of creating an internal function or using external services are not mutually exclusive, and except in cases where a firm chooses to rely entirely on external services, the proper mix of the two is that most likely to prove rewarding. There are parallels here with the other professional services which firms from time to time require and which are outside the main streams of their operations. Legal, patent and insurance departments, for example, commonly maintain continuing working relationships with their private counterparts. Perhaps marketing research is still too young for its inherent characteristics to be fully comprehended, but whereas it would be unusual for a solicitor within an industrial company to assume that he could look after that firm's total legal requirements without external assistance, it is still common for market researchers in industry to believe that they can handle all assignments and never require assistance from outside. Perhaps there is some failure to appreciate the distinction between the kind of specialist service which can be built up internally, scope and extent of services available from agencies whose continued existence depends on their operation as cohesive production units.

External considerations

The business environment of the firm may also determine the desirability of an internal function. In constantly changing situations associated, for example, with operating in areas of rapidly advancing technology; with serving markets where product life-cycles tend to be short; with periods of rapid growth or diversification, or with increasingly competitive markets, it is often too costly to rely completely on external services. Here the need is for careful monitoring on a continuous basis, and this is more economically carried out within the firm, with help sought from outside as occasion demands.

There is one other situation in which research is best contracted out. This is where the management is not wholly confident in internal professional services and will consequently be guarded in the acceptance, let alone adoption of recommendations from such sources. Reassurance in these situations can be provided only by obtaining supporting advice from outside.

Special considerations

Even when an in-company capability has been established there is a variety of reasons why external support must occasionally be considered. Sometimes the workload of the established department is such that it cannot handle a new assignment for which time is of the essence. Occasionally workloads can be rearranged and scheduling extended to permit high priority being given to new and urgent requirements, but in many cases this would mean displacing research that was itself urgent. Here an internal function that establishes a smooth working relationship with an outside agency is most fortunately placed in relation to its prime aim which is to serve management in a timely fashion.

There are other instances where even when the internal workload permits, there must be recourse to outside services. When it is imperative that a firm's identity should not be revealed during the course of a project it is inadvisable for it to attempt to undertake fieldwork itself. Its own staff cannot be sent into the field with an instruction to refuse to reveal the identity of their employer, nor must they ever be permitted to assume false or misleading identities. In contrast a research consultant, or an agency, can ethically refuse to reveal the identity of the client, and the choice of cooperation then rests entirely with the respondent.

There are no reasons for assuming that consultants or agency staff are less human than researchers employed in industry, and thus theoretically there should be no difference in the degree of objectivity attainable by both. For the most part, however, internal researchers are appreciably more involved in the day-to-day problems of the firm and may, dependent on the status of the research function within the firm, be liable to bias. When maximum objectivity is crucial, a marginal case can be made for preferring external services.

Sometimes, too, specialist skills are needed for the successful execution of research. These can range from mechanical skills, such as those necessary for the proper acquisition, handling and processing of large quantities of data, through those of the kind needed for motivational research, marketing research with a high operational research content, and the like. Again a firm may be seeking a depth study of a homogeneous market new to it, and here specialist services available from an agency with a history of successful research over an appreciable period in the specified market can ease the problem appreciably. In cases of this kind, it is usually uneconomic for manufacturing firms to build up their own specialist resources. Moreover, the need for them is usually infrequent.

Multi-client studies

Whether or not a firm has its own research facilities, there is one type of service offered by some agencies which can be immensely useful. Multiclient studies are on offer from time to time, and whilst it must be acknowledged that these often represent for the subscribing firms only the first phase of an overall research exercise, they do offer relatively low cost means of engaging in some research exercises which would otherwise be prohibitively costly for an individual firm. It is important, however, to appreciate from the outset the limitations of multiclient studies if disappointment is to be avoided in the final stages. Studies sponsored co-operatively can rarely, if ever, be sufficiently specific to the problems of an individual firm. However, if this restriction is fully appreciated, then provided the research is of the requisite calibre, an opportunity is offered that, on cost grounds alone, would not otherwise be available.

Making a short list of agencies

Over the last decade many firms have progressed from a total lack of awareness of any research requirement to a stage where, having made the decision as to the best method of coping with their needs, the most difficult remaining problem is how to select from the various research services available.

Through time, buying research must become a professional skill matching other industrial purchasing skills, but its importance and its necessary quality are perhaps still insufficiently appreciated. It is always more difficult to buy services than products because the latter can be specified so much more precisely, and often in quantifiable terms. Perhaps buying research services has most in common with placing orders for products only just into development and not yet in production: the end products on offer cannot be prejudged.

Once there has been successful and satisfying purchase of research services, the problem is immeasurably eased for the future. There should be nothing capricious in buying any professional service. There is little sense in change only for the sake of change – such attitudes are best left for hats and back-chat. These maxims do not, however, help the sponsor buying research for the first time, and his first task is to check all the available services which have prima facie suitability.

Somewhat at variance with the usual objective attitude recommended for all aspects of research, subjective judgements made by others often provide the best first indicators. Diligent enquiry will reveal business associates with research buying experience, and some of these will be prepared to comment frankly on their experiences, whether these be good or ill. Market research departments of other firms are usually willing to offer advice, and here the calibre of the market research department is the best guide as to whether or not such advice can be relied upon. Such professional bodies as banks, and trade and research associations are often also well placed in this context. Members of professional organisations like the Institute of Marketing and the British Institute of Management have access to lists of research services which have been compiled with appreciable care and with some investigation of the merits of these services before they are deemed to warrant inclusion in the lists.

Evaluating agencies

Having by one, or a combination of methods, selected at least three research services for further investigation, these must then be evaluated using some sort of screening process. Whilst there may be no immediate intention to buy research, but only to ensure preparedness for the speedy commissioning of future projects, much preliminary screening can still be carried out.

In the first place, the services selected as likely to be of interest should be asked to submit literature describing the scope of their operations and giving details of the resources at their command. Any published material, such as reprints of papers or articles, is well worth studying because from such publications it is often possible to judge something of the calibre of the services on offer. There is a parallel here with a practice common in the engagement of scientific and technical staff, where it has long been customary for references to published material to be submitted at the time applications for employment are made. Care must, of course, be exercised to ensure that the authors of the publications are still employed within the service, particularly when the papers submitted are of attractively high standard.

After study of the submitted literature, it should be possible to determine any restrictions in the probable capabilities of the service. It may show that past experience has been substantially concentrated in specific product/market areas or in highly specialized kinds of studies. For the most part, such restrictions are deliberately spelled out because it is the consultant's intention to limit the offer of his services to those areas where he has a competence of such an order that it gives him an edge over competitors. Provided there is a match between such specialist capabilities and the firm's requirements, the identification of services of this kind can be most rewarding for the client. In contrast, there are agencies, usually the larger ones, that are more broadly based and it must be recognized that the wider the scope of a competent agency's operations, the broader will have been its experiences and the more numerous the contacts it has made across the broad spectrum of industry. Capabilities of this extent are invaluable in many industrial marketing research investigations where a proper understanding of inter-industry links is vital to the solution of the problem prompting the research.

Few firms today rely only on home markets and thus an agency's links with overseas research companies, with associate consultants, or with subsidiaries overseas may be of special relevance. When it comes to the point of actually commissioning research, there must be careful scrutiny of such links because there can sometimes be a conflict of interest between the agency's clients and those of its affiliates.

In these first stages of screening, it is important to obtain comprehensive information on the number of people employed within an agency, their educational backgrounds and their qualifications. Many agencies, of course provide such data in their promotional literature.

Thus it is possible to build up reference files of data on external research services, but when the stage is reached of going out to tender for a research project, it is essential that the selected services be visited at their own premises. Just as in business and industry generally, much can be judged by careful and visual observation of the environment, in physical and sociological terms, in which the firm operates, so can similar observations aid in assessing the calibre and capability of a service organization. Impoverishment in regard to staff, equipment and furniture rarely promises well in the context of the ability to offer a competent marketing research service.

Before requesting a formal research proposal, it is wise after indicating the subject of the research which it is proposed to commission, to request information on past and present clients and on the kinds of projects handled. No reputable agency or consultant will refuse such a request, and in most cases the information will be offered without being asked for. This offers another opportunity for a potential sponsor to check with someone who has previously bought research, in this case specifically from the service under consideration. It is not unusual for past clients to be much more frank in giving their assessments of agency proficiency to another potential research sponsor than they would be in commenting directly to the agency: such is the cowardice of man.

Research proposals

Having taken all this care in initial selection it is imperative before actual commissioning that a formal research proposal or design be requested. The subject of briefing so that there can be expectation of a realistic proposal from which can be judged the capability of the consultant, and the probable standard of the ultimate research findings, is a subject in itself and cannot be elaborated here, but it is a cardinal rule that the more precise the brief, particularly in terms of the information requirements and the intended use of the research yield, the higher the probability that the research design, and ultimately the research programme and its results, will be satisfactory.

On the first two or three occasions when marketing research is being commissioned, it is important to obtain at least two quotations. On subsequent occasions the client may have developed sufficient confidence in a particular agency for this to be unnecessary. However, assuming that alternative quotations and research designs have been submitted, it is necessary to compare them. No research design is acceptable unless it spells out clearly the objectives and parameters of research, the anticipated research yield, the proposed form of the final research report, the research methods and the time and cost needed to achieve the specified results. Only when this has been done with a high degree of precision, is it possible for the research sponsor to judge whether the proposed design promises to meet his end requirements.

The guidelines indicated here, and much more beside, were originally set out in a chapter entitled " 'Make or Buy' in Marketing Research" in Aubrey Wilson's book: *The Assessment of Industrial Markets*; published by Hutchinson (1968). Only additional discourse has been contributed here, but if plagiary can be seen as flattery, perhaps the original author's indulgence may be gained.

2

BRIEFING A
MARKET RESEARCH AGENCY

The key to getting the best out of a market research agency is correct briefing. The textbooks deal with the nuts and bolts of the process; this article takes a look at some less obvious points. In order to write it, Stephen Marks took expert advice from both sides of the client/agency fence.

The principal function of market research is to assist managerial decision-making. It is therefore essential that a company's decision-making processes and the nature of the decisions likely to face management when the research has been completed, should be very much in mind during the briefing process. It is also essential for the research agency to know the background and objectives of the client if a correct interpretation of his research needs is to be arrived at. Without this it is likely that the research results will be irrelevant to the client's real problems and the result will be a lasting disenchantment with research.

Importance of mutual understanding

These are the main reasons why briefing and the subsequent drawing-up of detailed terms of reference are the most vital stages in any market research project. It is particularly important where a company is using market research for the first time. Here, the need for research, and the understanding of it, may well be limited. In such a case research may well be seen as an extra-ordinary expense by the company, unlike other items for which regular provision is made; this only increases the importance of achieving mutual understanding between agency and client in order to prevent subsequent disillusion.

Two hypothetical but all-too-typical examples show the pitfalls of failing to achieve this understanding at the briefing stage. A construction materials company decided it "needed some research done". It called in five agencies for an hour apiece "to discover their ideas". The agencies knew as little of the research plans of the company as the company itself. They made their representations to a company committee of 15 which had no idea what it wanted before it met, and precious few thereafter. The committee had no pretence of any standard by which to measure the agency presentations, and as the agencies knew that they had only one chance in five of getting the job, none of them felt like taking too much trouble over its presentation.

In another case, a company with a relatively clear idea of what it wanted, called in an agency for discussions. The company was left to go away and write its own brief. And the client was surprised when the final specification drawn up by the agency provided for research that could have cost over £50 a day. The moral? The final document should be one to which both sides have contributed a substantial amount; there are dangers in leaving too much to one side or the other. The process leading up to the briefiing can thus be as important as the briefing itself.

Which markets should be researched

The paradox of market research is that in a competitive business environment what each firm does, and needs to do, depends on the present and future actions of its competitors. The result is a competitive spiral of mutual action and reaction which may move so fast that in many cases a firm cannot afford to postpone the taking of crucial decisions until after the results of research are available; research which may well be outdated by the time it appears. In the words of Alan Hedges, research and marketing director of S. H. Benson, "you can't stop the world and say you want to find out what's happening". It is possible to avoid the twin dangers of taking too long on research and of eschewing it altogether and relying on good old-fashioned hunches. But this means facing up to the problem of trying to decide which products and problems can usefully be researched without the subject changing out of all recognition by the time the findings are available.

An on-going relationship is preferable

Another flaw in many companies' approach to the question of which problems to research is to imagine that the problem alone determines the kind of research needed, whereas the type of company decision-making involved can be just as important. The type of research needed to back up a new-product development for example, will be affected by just why the company needs to expand.

For all these reasons, many market researchers feel that ideally the briefing should not be a separate activity but part of an on-going relationship with an agency, on a regular account basis, not simply through one-off jobs. With a continuing relationship the briefing can be an organic process grown naturally from it. This avoids the more wasteful aspects of tendering, and is also more economic from the client's point of view. "The object", says Eileen Cole of Unilever's Research Bureau Ltd., "is not to tell them how to do the research, but what the problem is – or what the symptoms are."

Nevertheless, for many firms without previous experience of the use of market research, a start has to be made somewhere. A firm may be thrown into research by an isolated problem, and be convinced it knows exactly what research is needed to solve it. But if it sticks stubbornly to its own preconception of the problem, it will miss out on the benefit of discussing at length with the agency just what research's best contribution to the company's problems can be. And if a firm is in too much of a hurry for a reply to its own predetermined questions, pressure of time may make it uncritical of the information it is getting.

The importance of spelling out strategy

In order to be able to state clearly just what the problem is, the firm must be able to outline its present strategy. This is best done in terms of the company's total marketing plans; in the case of new product development for example, details of the existing range are essential.

"It helps", says Liz Nelson of Taylor Nelson and Associates, "to know what he knows about who he's selling to". This means giving agencies help on target markets. And full facilities for desk research, as well as any past research, must be made available. Desk research is rarely used enough, and can often save money. If the client has made fully clear just what the expected uses of the research are, the research agency can then produce recommendations on the actual research methodology, showing how the marketing objectives of the company can be met by the research planned. If the full proposals are drawn up, each area of the planned research can then be linked to one of the company's objectives.

Clarity on the crucial questions of client plans and the purpose of the research can affect the structure of the research itself. The degree of accuracy and detail required for initial appraisal of a major capital project might be quite different to what would be required in deciding on a mere enlargement of existing capacity, reorganization of sales territories, or establishing what customers think of the product or the company. And each extra unit of accuracy can cost disproportionately more. If 70 per cent accuracy can be obtained for £X, while 90 per cent accuracy could cost £5X, it is obviously important to decide at the outset if 70 per cent accuracy is sufficient for the purpose in hand.

The agency needs to know not only the purposes for which the information is needed, but also how much freedom of action is allowed by the company's decision-making structure. This reinforces again the need for a long-term relationship with a market research company so that a firm can get to the position where the agency itself volunteers suggestions as to what research may be required in future, and where an agency executive will be naturally included from the beginning as a member of a new product team. Such a situation may seem the next-best thing to having one's own research department.

Briefing for fieldwork only

Those firms that do have their own research staff often get to the point where they use agencies simply to buy the fieldwork. Kodak, for example, maintains two market research departments, one for the consumer division and one for industrial research. On the consumer side, so consumer research head David Nobbs told us, Kodak goes to an agency with a clearly explained outline of research requirements already prepared. All it requires from the agency is the collection of the information, which Kodak then interprets for itself, sometimes even giving the agency a set of blank tables for the presentation of the results. At special meetings, Kodak will go through the questionnaire and suggest alterations. The agency will also be briefed on the method of fieldwork and type of sample. "We like to insist on a pilot survey, ' says Nobbs, 'and we have on occasion sent our own men out to check; we do at least insist on an executive of the agency going out on the pilot." The company also insists on meeting the researchers and interviewers who will work on the assignment. And in the industrial research division, where much research is highly technical in nature, they have even organized training sessions for the agency interviewing staff. "We intervene in the running of the survey as much as we like," says industrial research head David Figg, "in fact we're a bloody nuisance."

The dangers of narrow briefing

Some large agencies like Marplan and AGB are now setting up subsidiaries to cater specially for firms requiring this "fieldwork only" service. But for firms without the same internal research resources, the problem arises of how tightly to brief the agency. How detailed should the brief be, and how narrowly tied down to what the commissioning company sees as actionable? The danger here is that by insisting on too narrow a brief, the company could lose the benefit of an agency's outside view of the firm's own definition of its problems. A problem can often seem specific only because a company has not thought about it in a different way.

The recent emphasis on an "action-oriented philosophy" carries with it the danger that only those problems will be researched on which the company feels that decisions can be taken. But this is to assume that the alternatives between which a choice has to be made are fixed in advance of the research, rather than illuminated or even altered in the light of its findings. The danger to be avoided is that action-oriented research can be much easier to set up the more trivial it is, while the more fundamental questions may not convert so easily and directly into obviously actionable terms. For example, a company which, after a takeover, finds itself marketing a product in a blue package in the north of the country and in a red one in the south, might think it obvious and straightforward to settle by simple consumer surveys which of the two is most effective for national use. An agency might suggest, however, that the most appropriate subject for research was the total packaging policy of the company. Again, the border between actionable and non-actionable research is something that will vary with the overall activities and strategy of the firm, thus reinforcing the need for close co-operation with the agency over time.

"Anyway," asks Alan Hedges, "what are non-actionable data? Sometimes it may mean that the person making the statement has a low opinion of his own ability to act. But other people can be stimulated by anything. Most research doesn't make life easier, it makes it more difficult." The brief, he thinks, should stimulate the research people, clarify the problem, and specify any pre-determined limits for the conclusion. Within those limits, if the research company more or less writes its own brief, the client is then getting a valuable input from the agency, which it would not get with a narrower brief.

Eileen Cole makes a similar point. "At the briefing stage, you must have standards which the client is going to operate to; courses of action he will take, and might take if certain results are achieved." The agency can then clearly point out if those standards have been reached or not, whatever else it may turn up in the course of the research. The agency should also recommend whatever else it thinks necessary, so long as the facts and the interpretation are kept separate.

When the final brief is in the agency's hands, it can go off and prepare a detailed proposal. This is in fact a specification of the research to be undertaken. It should be agreed to by both sides, and is an opportunity to confirm that there are no potentially disastrous misunderstandings between client and agency. If management has not taken the researchers sufficiently into its confidence, or if the researchers have failed to enquire deeply into the purposes for which the research is required, the resulting mis-understandings may come to light only when it is too late. A typical and widely repeated example of this is the manufacturer who demanded information on "market shares" of his product, when in fact what he wanted to know was the quantities of the product he could sell at given price levels; a totally different piece of research. It is particularly important, especially where highly technical products or overseas markets are involved, that there should be clear and mutually accepted definitions of customer types, product groups, and geographical areas.

Avoiding misunderstandings

A useful means of reducing to a minimum the possibilities of such misunderstanding is for the agency to go on a "trip round the works", with researchers going round whatever aspect of the manufacturing process or the company's organization, is relevant to the subject of the research. Thus in a research project on an aspect of, or including, the packaging, design and presentation of the product, the researchers could with advantage spend at least a day with the design department of the client company, learning how the "language" and conceptual approach of the design department differs from that of the consumers.

Exchanges in the opposite direction are also advantageous. Surprisingly few clients ask to go out with field workers or enquire in any detail about the technical details of the research. Here again, a continuing "consultancy relationship" provides an environment in which this is more likely to be possible than in a "one-off job" approach, which Eileen Cole compares to approaching an ad agency for a single commercial.

The agency's ability to inspire trust is of course crucial in any relationship in which the client is not to keep the researchers at arm's length, a course of action which as we have seen can be costly in the long run. A firm which feels it cannot trust its agency fully with information about the purposes of the research and the course of action open to it should get itself another agency; and an agency which was not worthy of being trusted with such information would certainly find it difficult to get another client.

The importance of keeping continuing contact

The final brief should not be the end of continuous contact between client and researchers throughout the life of the project. Of course each side should immediately inform the other of any changes affecting the original plans – if, for example, the agency finds it is getting a lower rate of strike than expected, or weather makes calls difficult.

More fundamental revisions may become necessary in the course of the research. This is especially likely where, as is common in the consumer field, the research is organized as a two-stage project, in which the first stage preceding an actual survey, consists of qualitative research – that is to say research based on indirect non-quantitative methods such as depth interviews and group discussions. At the end of each stage client and agency should ask each other if the research is still meeting the original objectives. Revision may often be necessary, especially where the project involves advertising. For example, a research firm was asked by a client in the pharmaceuticals field to prepare a report on the relative acceptability to the market of 11 different advertising concepts. After the completion of a group discussion stage, the agency gave an interim report-back to the client. It felt unable to go further unless the client could decide which of two target groups discovered by the research up to that point, it wished to go for. But the agency did feel that if it could cut the total number of concepts down to five or six, it could then get down to the chosen target group, and decide which of, say, three concepts best appealed to it.

Agencies are not averse to this sort of continuing consultation.

As Liz Nelson put it, "Agencies used to go away for four months and come back with 'the answer'. But it doesn't happen like that any more, thank God." There is a difference, however, between amending the brief in the direction of greater precision in the light of the first-stage findings, and alterations due to a simple change of mind or intention on the part of the client. Revision on this scale is usually a mistake.

The brief and the research findings

Finally, how should the brief be reflected in the presentation of the final findings? While the final brief itself should be explicit about which questions it wants answered, it should also permit, or even require, the agency to report in as much detail as it may find necessary on any other aspects relevant to the marketing of the product which may come to light in the course of the research. The facts and the agency's interpretation of them should, however, be kept separate. Thus the client can benefit from the experience of the agency (many of the larger and older-established agencies offer a consultancy service as part of the package), while leaving the client's own research and marketing departments free to come to their own conclusions, if different, on the basis of the evidence submitted.

3
ESTIMATING MARKET SIZE

Leslie Walsh of PA Consultants examines some of the problems of estimating industrial market size and gives practical advice on sources, limitations and cross-checking.

Your managing director leans forward earnestly: "You do understand. We don't want an expensive job. Just do some quick research and tell us the size of the market and other such basic essentials. That's all we want."

The industrial market researcher has long ago learnt to accept such a remark with stoic patience. In his experience, requests of this nature are not unusual. So many competent and successful industrial executives – even marketing executives – seem to have a blind spot when it comes to estimating market size. They fail to understand just how difficult and expensive it can sometimes be.

Let us leave aside for the moment the question of whether market size is a "basic essential" – except to say that it sometimes is not – and examine the various methods of assessing the size of industrial markets.

Secondary Sources

First of all, in many situations our managing director is right: a little simple desk research may well be all that is required. Government and quasi-government statistics are themselves a very fruitful source of information. It must also be borne in mind that government departments can publish only a part of the data they collect, simply because publication of the whole would be quite uneconomic. A telephone call to the relevant department or ministry can often solve apparently insurmountable problems. (This does not apply, of course, to commercial information supplied on a confidential basis, which is subject to very strict safeguards.)

The managing director will also point to the 1967 Companies Act: "Surely it is easier now to assess market size, since turnover must be disclosed?" But the Act, unfortunately, is by no means as helpful as market researchers might have hoped. It permits directors to treat as one class "classes of business which, in the opinion of the directors, do not differ substantially from each other" – a provision of which many directors take full advantage.

Trade associations are often helpful, though not invariably so. And while *any* published statistics must be carefully scrutinized and cross-checked for accuracy, this is doubly important with trade association figures. Among the more common pitfalls are incompleteness of membership, radical changes of membership, changes in product definitions and inadequate methods of analysis; among the more exotic dangers are the rare instances of falsification of returns by members.

Even if desk research produces no information of direct relevance, it is often possible to deduce market size from indirectly related figures. The most obvious and straightforward examples occur in components, where sales figures for the finished product give clear guidance. More complicated, but still reliable, relationships can often be established quite cheaply, and there is scope for some ingenuity.

Nevertheless, despite this wealth of published and available unpublished information, there remains a vast number of markets and products on which there is just no information, and where original research becomes essential.

Original Research

Special problems

Industrial research often presents special problems not encountered in consumer work. With major items of capital equipment. for instance, a single year's purchase figures can be quite misleading, owing to the relative infrequency of purchase or to the strongly cyclic nature of demand. A possible solution is to average demand over the last five years, or over whatever period appears suitable in the light of the product life cycle. This does, however, considerably increase the difficulty of field work – much more is demanded of informants and interviewers.

In certain circumstances, it may be more practicable to direct enquiries at the age and total stock of equipment, and to deduce current and future markets by the use of actuarial techniques. However, let us limit ourselves to the less difficult and perhaps more usual situations.

Complete coverage

In certain industrial markets our managing director is still in the right: in some cases the total number of customers and potential customers is so small that all can be interviewed at limited cost. However, difficulties now begin to arise: not all informants are prepared to co-operate. With so few informants, even one or two refusals could render any assessment of market size impossible.

Alternative approach areas

In some industrial markets, however, the number of customers and potential customers for the product under survey is often so high that any attempt to approach them all would be wildly uneconomic. In this situation the first instinct of the industrial market researcher is to move up the chain of industrial demand – from end-users to distributors or from end-users to original equipment manufacturers. Alternatively, he might even move sideways, to competing manufacturers. In this way, of course, the numbers of informants, and hence the cost of the survey, can be drastically reduced.

Such an approach is not always possible, however, For instance, many industrial products are not sold through distributors. Even where they are, distributors are usually among the most difficult of informants. Not unnaturally, they regard the market information they have as a valuable asset in their business, and confidential to themselves. They are, again quite reasonably, unwilling either to undertake the clerical work which many market surveys involve, or to make their sales records available to a market research analyst.

Competitors deserve a special mention. They could, by co-operating, reduce the cost of a survey to the level contemplated by our managing director. Most research consultancies will approach competitors as a matter of routine, often with an offer of some exchange of information, and the approach can be surprisingly successful. It must, however, be made openly and the fact that the sponsor is a competitor must be made known (any other approach is unethical and will not be countenanced by any reputable consultancy). In any case, the information provided must never be accepted without cross-checks. Not all competitors will take the trouble to provide really accurate information, and cases of deliberate attempts to mislead are not unknown.

Random and quota sampling

Thus there are still very many situations where the industrial researcher is faced with vast numbers of potential informants. It is then that our managing director suggests – on the face of it, not unreasonably – some form of random sampling. After all, he has possibly been well served in the past by consumer research agencies who have provided, at very reasonable cost, market data with statistical validation. Why can't these industrial fellows do the same?

The first difficulty is the statistical requirement that for a true random sample every item in the relevant population must have exactly the same chance of election as any other item. This means, in industrial research terms, that a complete list must be prepared of all establishments relevant to the survey before sample selection can take place.

There may well be many thousands of such establishments, and certain leading directories or credit control services, such as Kompass and Dun and Bradstreet, offer at very reasonable cost a computer service that no industrial market researcher can afford to ignore. The cost of preparation of a complete list of all establish-ments relevant to the survey, however, can still be quite un-economic in many cases. The consumer researcher, in contrast, has access to the electoral register, at negligible cost. Admittedly, this is not itself perfect – recently it even included a few horses, according to press reports – but it is more than adequate for all practical purposes. The industrial researcher would give his ears for an industrial counterpart, horses and all.

Just as fundamental a difficulty in the use of random sampling (though one more easily overcome) is the lack of homogeneity in most industrial markets: certain companies offer vastly greater potential than others. Imagine the results obtainable from a random sample of the chemical industry which happened not to include ICI.

If the consumer researcher finds a random sample unnecessary or impracticable, he can turn to quota sampling. The process is simple, and, with adequate field control, reliable: the interviewer simply selects likely informants until he has built up to a predetermined quota. Building up the quota may not be as easy as it might seem, but there is a wealth of demographic information available as a basis, much of it, such as the Census of Population, provided at vast government expense. There is nothing like the equivalent in industrial fields.

Thus, although industrial researchers do use, when appropriate, sampling methods akin to random and quota sampling, only rarely can any degree of statistical validation be attached to the results. It should not be imagined that the profession as a whole is satisfied with this state of affairs: much research is being undertaken. For the time being, however, our managing director must often be disappointed.

Lorenz distribution situations

The general lack of homogeneity in industrial markets has already been commented upon. Often a Lorenz distribution situation exists (i.e. by far the greater part of purchases is usually accounted for by a relatively small number of companies). In these circumstances a high proportion of the market can be identified in comparatively few interviews. The industrial market researcher, as a matter of routine, will take full advantage of this situation.

In this way a definite minimum size of market can be clearly identified. This may very well prove adequate for the business decision to be made.

For example, in a decision to build a new factory, it is rare for market size to be the only constraint. If availability of finance limits the factory to a certain maximum size, and therefore output, there is no real point in spending money on market research beyond the point at which it has located a size of market adequate to allow every chance that the full output will be sold.

It can be unwise to rely too heavily, however, on the Lorenz approach. Not only are the results obviously biased to big-company practices, but smaller companies may prove easier to penetrate, quality demands may not be so exacting, price levels may prove more remunerative, and purchasing policies less strict. It may prove unwise to entrust all the industrial eggs to too few industrial baskets. For these reasons, even if the Lorenz approach locates an adequate market, the industrial researcher will also approach a number of smaller companies, as a general rule.

But what if the Lorenz approach fails to locate anything like an adequate size of market? And what about situations where Lorenz does not apply? There are, for instance, many thousands of laboratories in this country, but for certain products only the Department of Health and Social Security purchases in really significant quantities. In other cases, the survey may be directed specifically at smaller companies.

It may be thought, after a discussion of so many alternative approaches, that such situations are rare, but this is not the case. The industrial researcher is not infrequently faced with a situation in which the most he can hope for is a broad approximation, though usually this is supported by safeguards in the form of correlation tests, broad market assessments using an alternative base.

Making a broad market assessment

In the case of each user industry, both during desk research and during field work, the researcher endeavours to locate some factors which:

(a) can be related to reliable published data covering the industry as a whole;

(b) also bear a reasonably close and consistent relationship to purchases, by establishments in the sample, of the products under investigation.

The approach is perhaps best illustrated by taking one of the most commonly accepted indicators – numbers of employees. The calculation might be expressed in its crudest form as follows:

$$\text{Estimated industry purchases} = \frac{\text{Total numbers employed in relevant SIC* category} + \text{Purchases of the survey product by informant establishments}}{\text{Total numbers employed in informant establishments}}$$

It will be realized that this particular approach is based on two principal assumptions. First, that establishments' purchases of the product under survey are proportionate to size of establishment, and second, that size is adequately measured for this purpose by numbers of employees.

On the face of it these appear to be eminently commonsense assumptions. A few seconds further thought, however, will show that a number of dangers are inherent in this approach. The extent of mechanization/automation, or the ratio of indirect/direct employees, can radically affect the value of the employee indicator. Further, establishments are usually classified to only one SIC category, that which accounts for the greater part of their production; yet it is, of course, not unusual for a single establishment to manufacture several different products covering several SIC categories. Some allowance must also be made for establishments which manufacture the survey product as a secondary line, and are thus classified to other SIC categories. Finally, while the industrial researcher is now working necessarily by establishments, companies' purchasing policies may be partially or wholly centralized at head offices and may relate to the enterprise as a whole.

Clearly, to accept blindly the approach outlined in the example would be a highly dangerous proceeding. Some of the dangers, however, can be eliminated by really competent field work, while the basic assumptions can be checked to a large extent by correlation tests. Usually data will be adequate for simple tests of linear correlation, and on really major surveys it may be possible to investigate further for non-linear relationships. Often there will be no real need even for this degree of sophistication. The existence of a reasonable straight-line relationship (between establishment's purchases and the number of employees at the establishment) can be checked merely by plotting on a graph.

Whether or not the employee indicator provides a satisfactory correlation, it is important to use as many other indicators as possible, in order to provide cross-checks. Possible indices are turnover, output in quantity terms, raw material consumption, or rateable values. Each of these is applicable to certain situations. Many other indicators are possible, depending on the product under survey – there is again scope for ingenuity.

To sum up, the use of such indicators, with adequate field work, proper safeguards, cross-checks against background control data, and just a modicum of common sense and experience, offers an additional method of arriving at a reasonable estimate of market size. So far, where direct comparison of methods has proved possible, results have been satisfactory.

Such indicators are, of course, the last resort after all other approaches have failed. What happens if these methods, too, fail to give satisfactory results?

In such cases, our managing director must simply face the unpalatable fact that in certain industrial market research situations it is just not possible to obtain at economic cost any reliable estimate of market size.

It may, ironically, be of some consolation to him to know that professional industrial researchers themselves are in the same boat. Despite praiseworthy efforts by some practitioners, the industrial researcher is still woefully short of reliable data on the market for his own services.

Reference

Standard Industrial Classification: the Government's classification of trade and industry, designed to promote uniformity and comparability in official statistics. Copies of the Classification are obtainable from HMSO.

4
CREATING PRODUCTS THAT CREATE CUSTOMERS

The product is not what the factory makes; it is what the customer buys. Theodore Levitt, Professor of Business Administration at the Harvard Business School, is best known through his article "marketing myopia". Here he shows that even the business lunch is part of the product, and the point of sale is a point of production.

When asked some years ago what his company did, Charles Revson, the perfectionist president of Revlon, offered a profound distinction: "In the factory we make cosmetics; in the store we sell hope."

He obviously has no illusions. He knows that chastity is the rarest of all sexual aberrations. People don't buy things – goods or services. They buy the expectations of benefits: not cosmetics, but the allurements they create for their users; not quarter-inch drills, but quarter-inch holes; not common stocks, but capital gains; not numerically controlled milling machines, but trouble-free and accurately smooth parts; not Dream Whip dessert, but sophisticated convenience.

What the product really is

This means that the definition of a product comes not from its generic essence, but from the problems people are trying to solve with it. A teenager may refer to his car as "wheels", but he uses it for the freedom it bestows and for the opportunities it confers on him with the girls. An underwriting may be what a Wall

Street firm produces, but the firm whose name is on the prospectus is buying the utilities bestowed by the expected money.

A product is not something people consume. It is a tool they use. The object of consumption is to solve a problem. Even consumption that is directed at the creation of an opportunity – like going to Medical School or taking a one-way trip to the Caribbean – is purposefully oriented toward solving a problem. At a minimum, the medical student seeks to solve the problem of how to lead a relevant and comfortable life. The lady on the tour seeks to solve the problem of spinsterhood.

This view holds that a product is not what the engineer explicitly says it is, but what the consumer implicitly says.

The significance of that distinction is anything but trivial. Nobody knows this better than the people who create automobile ads. It is not the generic virtues that they extol, but more likely the car's capacity to enhance its user's status and his access to female prey. Not far removed is the strategy of the project manager for a sophisticated missile guidance system.

It is not over blueprints and test results that the project manager pores with his Pentagon guest at enormously overpriced and elegantly underlighted Washington restaurants. Instead, he pours bourbon over ice while talking more about the pennant race than the space race. His object is more to create a personal relationship of trust and an institutional obligation toward his company than to transmit solid information about his generic product.

What the missile project manager does in Washington is no different than what is done by the machine tool designer in Worcester. While the former tries to impress and obligate the prospect by feeding him on a relentless diet of strong whisky and heroic stories of his company's R & D prowess and delivery reliability, the latter does essentially the same by trying with colour, sculptured edges, a fancy control panel, and false perspective to make an ordinary six-spindle lathe look like a computerized technotron of awesome superiority and reliability.

Or take the case of a new $700 electronics laboratory testing device. It yielded twice as many purchase intentions from Ph.D. laboratory directors when its front panel was redesigned by a professional *designer than when it was designed by the development engineers. The holders of Ph.D. degrees in electrical engineering from the Massachusetts Institute of Technology were thus quite as responsive in their laboratories to the blandishments of packaging as Mr Revson's fragile ladies at the "hope" counter in the stores.*

The customer is not king

A product is more than its generic essence. What counts is how the customer views it. And that is something over which the producer and the seller have more control than meets the eye. Only people in the iron grip of cultural lag, or those hopelessly befuddled by the homilies of obsolete moralizers believe that the customer is king. He may have the last word as to whether or what he will buy, but he is not exempt from the influence of the seller.

The assumption that the consumer can be influenced is the basis of all promotion. But it is a point few men in business dare make out loud in public. It has a manipulative and devious ring, presumably abrasive on the public ear, and, besides, not especially comforting to the speaker himself. He was told throughout childhood by his own wise and loving mother that honesty, kindness, fairness, truth, charity, and service to his fellow man are the ultimate human virtues. Obviously, things have changed a great deal since he left home. So if he cannot now lead a life of selfless service to humanity, he can certainly in his business life eschew deliberate deception and manipulation – or at least he can have the decency not to promote or justify their use by others.

The real morality of business

It is helpful if we divest ourselves of the spurious moralizing that is such a pathological part of the commercial rhetoric. To justify advertising and promotion, men in business tax their imaginations to the limit, spinning elaborately transparent webs of apology – always ultimately to the self-righteous effect that promotion is good for the economy because it creates jobs and raises living standards. No doubt all this frenzied rhetoric is a necessity imposed by the guilt of childhood remembrances – the endless lies about how beautifully the world works and about the selfless purposes of man that were so relentlessly drilled into all of us as children by our well-meaning mothers years ago. Now that as adults we lead lives so inescapably different from what mother said was proper, and since maternal wisdom heard at an early age, no matter how silly or downright false it may have been, has an almost immortal tenacity, we feel morally compelled somehow to justify those lives.

The resulting blather and fraudulence is enough to send an educated man over to the enemy. The fact is that the world is nothing like we were ever told. None of us can live our mothers' rigid fantasies. Nor would any of us really want to. What we want is to face life, not escape from it. And much of what seems in business to the thoughtless mind as trivial and extraneous is in fact the reality we both cherish and require for survival. The fact is that in bright promotion, exaggerated advertisements, elaborated packaging, puffy product design, and generous business lunches we have a more realistic and honest reflection of the nature of man and the reality of life than anything dear old mother was ever capable of contemplating. It is she who told the lies, and the ad man who tells the truth.

Truth is what man does, not what he says. And everywhere he does the same thing – he modifies, embellishes, rewrites, and re-packages an otherwise crude, vulgar, and oppressive reality. He does it in order that life might for the moment be made more tolerable. In commerce this is called advertising, industrial design, and packaging. In other professions it is called poetry, art, fashion, architecture, religion. The poet does not offer an engineering description of a Grecian urn – he offers an exaggerated, lyrical, palpably false description. His objective is quite the same as the ad man who lyricizes extravagantly about the latest model automobile. Both seek a heightening effect on the minds and emotions of their audiences.

Apostolic admen

Why have all the popes of history approved of the extravagant and costly architecture of St Peter's Basilica and the thousands of other places of worship around the globe? Is not the poetic imagery of Christ – a man of sackcloth and sandals – enough to inspire, elevate, and hold the flock together? Why embellish the house of God with the same elaborate fixturing and materialistic luxuries as go inside a Cadillac automobile? How is the advertisement of the inside of an automobile which makes it look as spacious as a king's palace any more dishonest and less honorable than the false perspective which gives such grandeur to Michelangelo's frescoes on the Sistine ceiling? Certainly it cannot be said that their objectives are different. Both seek to influence an audience – and, perhaps to stretch a point, the ad man does it with considerably less pretension. The ad man seeks only to convert the audience to his commercial custom. Michelangelo seeks to convert its soul.

The so-called distortions of advertising, design, packaging, and even business lunches are as essentially central parts of all products as wheels are essential parts of cars, as imagery is essential to poetry, and as decorative robes are essential for the priestly professions. A practising clergyman without distinctive and appropriately opulent robes to set him apart from lesser mortals would suffer in authority, credibility, and promise as much as a vial of perfume designed by Frankenstein or an IBM machine designed by Rube Goldberg.

Nor, as we saw, is the PhD engineer exempt from the influences of elaboration. He needs as many outer artefacts to provide reassurance for what he buys for his laboratory as the under-educated lady in the kitchen. To call some of the devices and embellishments employed to provide this reassurance by the pejorative name that is so commonly used, namely, "gimmicks", is not just silly; it is a denial of the things men honestly need and value. If religion must be architectured, packaged, lyricized, and set to music in order to attract and hold its audience, and if sex must be perfumed, powdered, corseted, sprayed, and shaped in order to sustain itself, then how can we deny the legitimacy of more modest similar embellishments in such a lesser world as commerce? It is more than silly to refer to such embellishments as silly. It can, in fact, be an error that can be enormously costly in business.

A promotion, or a clever ad, or an arresting package, or an attractive control panel, or even an elaborate lunch – these are essential features of the product because without them little or nothing would be sold. If a product is something somebody buys, then if it is not bought it cannot be said to exist – at least not commercially. If people buy the product promises they believe in, then whatever produces and sustains these promises is inherent to these products.

To make the point another way, consider the case of a chemical manufacturer who provides his customers, for no additional cost, with considerable technical services. Without these services there is the presumption that lots of present customers would simply not have bought the product, and certainly not this supplier's product if his competitors were supplying such services.

Nothing could be clearer than that the technical services are a central part of this company's product. Without them there would be no sales – certainly fewer sales. To suggest that they are peripheral to the generic product is not just to prefer a more limited or somehow a more tangible definition of what a product is: it is to make a grave error. The customer is trying to satisfy his needs, to solve a problem. Without technical services he either cannot solve it or does so at a greater cost to himself. Hence, technical services are part of what he buys. The same is true of industrial design in milling machines, fancy bottles in cosmetics, and the accounting firm's advertisements for itself via the publication of timely articles under the names of its principals.

What counts: the chemistry, not the chemical

In a world of increasing similarity and even standardization of generic products – from chemicals to steels, to cosmetics, to computers, to insurance policies, and even to political party platforms – what distinguishes one from the other are increasingly the customer-attracting and customer-satisfying related benefits with which the generic product is surrounded. These are why customers prefer one to another supplier. It is not the generic product that counts, but the cluster of benefits or value satisfactions with which the supplier surrounds the generic product. What counts is not the chemical but the chemistry – not the generic scientific thing for which the chemists have a highly impressive formula, but the satellite attributes attached to this central chemical but for which even businessmen too often have only contempt. We call them "gimmicks" or "just promotions" or "tailfins". Yet it is the latter that turn the customer on, that offer the distinguishing characteristics that produce patronage. Why do they produce patronage? Because it is these things that the customer values more than the generic content which he takes for granted.

The adman: today's poet

In a world where so many substantive things are either commonplace or standardized, it makes no sense to refer to the rest as false, fraudulent, frivolous, or immaterial. The world works according to the aspirations and needs of its actors, not according to the arcane, ordained, or moralizing logic of people who pine for another age – an age which, in any case, seems different from today's largely because of the fact that its observers were then children. In the world of adults, the seller has no choice but to try to understand the problems and aspirations of the actors to whom he directs his efforts, and then to try to find ways to hook on to these for his commercial advantage. Both sides will generally benefit from the effort. The heightening of expectations and the embellishment of life that are the objects of church architecture or T. S. Eliot are no more worthy for the sensibilities to which they appeal than the appeal to the senses we observe in William Bernbach's composition of advertising copy. "The product" is what people feel with their senses, not just sterile objects like granite, paint, steel, copper wire, and letters on a page. In both cases the artisan and the poet each correctly assumes that his audience requires more than sterile functionality.

Universal application of the concept

If in these highly personal ways a product is more than its rudimentary generic self, does it follow that in less personal situations this principle also holds? I think that clearly it does. Take the case of air cargo.

When American Airlines first concluded that almost anything was worth trying to put its fleet of idle planes to work between midnight and 7 a.m., it looked around for hitherto unexploited possibilities for air cargo. One possibility was to substitute fast overnight air deliveries from factories to customers for the same kind of fast service usually provided by regional warehouses located near the customers. American suggested this possibility to the Distributor Products Division of Raytheon Corporation, proposing the possibility of its eliminating its five regional warehouses. But American quickly discovered that to offer fast overnight delivery was not enough. Whereas customers could now call local warehouses by phone to get quick delivery, ordering from the factory entailed long communications delays if the orders went by mail, and high costs if phoned long distance. The solution was obviously to accelerate the placement and transmission of orders. For Raytheon to accept long-distance toll calls might have been a modest additional cost relative to the saving of warehouse eliminations and inventory investment, but then there were the high costs of handling and processing these small orders, making invoices where before customers bought off warehouse shelves, making shipping orders, and maintaining a complex central inventory control system.

Instead of dropping this problem into Raytheon's lap, American persuaded Western Union and the Friden Company to join with it in developing an elaborate but simplified communications and data processing system to handle these problems. Friden developed an automatic order-placing method using prepunched cards for each of Raytheon's products. A distributor could place these cards into a console and simply type out the number of desired units of the item represented by each card. Automatically this would register, via Western Union, at Raytheon's distant plant, where a reader-printer would instantly type out an invoice, a shipping order and shipping route, make inventory adjustments, and, upon reaching certain inventory check points, create a production order for inventory replenishment. Each evening American would assemble the orders at the factory for removal to its cargo terminal and over-night air shipment to the customer.

Having thus solved all the problems produced by the proposed warehouse eleminations, Raytheon quickly switched to air cargo.

It would be a terrible mistake to say that in this case Raytheon bought and American sold air cargo. Air cargo is a commodity that was used, but it is not the product that was either bought or sold. "The product" was the entire package that American, Western Union, and Friden assembled so ingeniously. Air cargo by itself could not have been sold. Raytheon was not interested in air cargo, and especially not if it created new problems of ordering and communication. Raytheon sought only to buy the solution to a problem. This required more than air cargo alone. The fashionable word for what it bought is a "system". The system was the product, not just its generic entity. By itself air cargo could not have been sold, any more than perfume in a sardine can.

Only beatniks and cannibals would think you could sell perfume in a sardine can. Everbody else knows that the package is a central part of the appeal that sells. But to acknowledge this for perfume imposes on us the need to consider how other "products" and services depend for their sales success in the same way on things other than the generic commodity they contain.

Even the lunch is part of the product

Consider the elaborate ballet performed several thousand times each day across the nation around the typical corporate purchasing agent. Whether he is in the market for pencils or pressure pumps, it is obligatory that the salesman who calls on him any time between 11.30 a.m. and noon seeks the pleasure of his company at lunch. There is a well-founded presumption that this offer – or its absence – will affect the chances of making the sale.

Only the totally uninformed or inexperienced critic would refer either to this gesture or to its fulfilment as a case of dignified white collar bribery. It is, in fact, a solidly sensible way in which the unfairly abused purchasing agent gets important information about the supplier, and in which the unkindly accused salesman tries to understand the needs and ways of the prospect while simultaneously providing the often subtle but necessary assurances about his company's reliability and good intentions. The fact that the lunch occurs in surroundings of elaborate opulence that reflect favourably on the good will of the supplier, that the participants do less poring over production specifications than they do pouring over ice, and that the conversation turns more to football than figures does not alter the fact of its being a meaningful, legitimate, and productive commercial and human encounter.

The very fact that the two parties talk in lengthy introductory detail about football, and exchange, like long-separated college room-mates, intimate details of their private family lives is significant. It is a device by which both parties test each other's integrity and reliability. A man with four thriving children, a loyal wife, two pedigree dogs, and a solid respect for the talents of Mr Joe Namath cannot be all bad When the purchasing agent then talks about his company's needs and buying methods, and when the salesman then extols the virtues of his pencils or the instant availability of his company's pump application specialists, there is now some reasonable basis for the two parties to believe each other. The salesman has, albeit unintentionally, enhanced to the purchasing agent the credibility of his claims It is now safer than it was before for the purchasing agent to consider buying the product. It will not arrive suspect and unacceptable in a sardine can. The lunch, like the paintings on the Sistine ceiling, obviously serves a useful purpose for both sides. Properly considered, the lunch is as much the product that was, as a consequence, exchanged as were the pencils themselves.

Production at the point of sale

One of the most visible yet least understood aspects of products is the extent to which they are produced at point of sale rather than in the factory. The infamous failure of Univac in the 1950s is a perfect example.

Univac had a well-functioning and highly touted computer on the market while the International Business Machines Corporation was still debating with itself whether the computer had enough market potential to justify a development effort. A dozen years later "IBM" was the generic synonym for the computer, and Univac was in shambles.

What happened is now clear enough. Univac sought to sell people computers made in the factory, while IBM sold people solutions to their problems. IBM's army of highly trained, customer-sensitive salesmen carefully analysed their prospects' problems and designed programs and management systems to solve these through the use of computers. Instead of suggesting that the computer was some sort of miraculous business liberator that would obsolete the past, thereby throwing its prospects into paroxysms of fear and hesitation, IBM suggested in great, reliable, and implementable detail exactly how the prospect's specific operations would benefit from the suggested computerization of his operations. And then IBM went further – it assumed solid responsibility for its own suggestions by doing itself all the numerous things in the prospect's offices, plants, and warehouses to enable him actually to switch to the computer.

The product the IBM customer bought obviously was not just the computer. That is what Univac, the pioneer producer, offered but could not sell. IBM customers bought a product whose significance consisted more in what was designed and produced at point of sale than at the factory.

5

A LICENCE FOR MORE PROFIT

If overseas markets are closed to your product by quotas or tariff barriers, or simply by the cost of transport, one way out could be to licence a foreign manufacturer to make, and even sell it for you. How it should be done is explained by Henry Deschampneufs.

To sell some £8,000 million of goods a year to overseas markets should make us feel proud of British exporters. It represents a higher total per head of population than from any other country. But still the cry goes up for more exports, because our share of total world trade is declining.

To this the harassed exporter will reply that there are many markets overseas that are closed to his products because of import restrictions, high customs tariffs and so on. He will add that in many markets local governments restrict imports in order to build up their own indigenous industries. And he will point out that because his product has to be altered to suit local preferences in many cases, this makes the development of such markets uneconomic. Where, he may ask, is his increased export trade to come from? And how can he compete with the ever-growing labour costs and raw material prices that threaten his company with being priced right out of many of his existing markets?

Part of the answer lies in British exporters increasing or developing their invisible earnings from overseas. It is only part of the answer because it would clearly not be in anyone's interest if every exporter concentrated on this side of export business to the exclusion of direct exports, as then there would be far less production, more unemployment, and a much smaller national earning power, along with the difficulties an industrial company would experience under such circumstances.

But where visible exports cannot be increased further because it is impossible to overcome tariff barriers and so on, then one has to consider manufacturing locally behind those barriers. This can be done by setting up a factory or subsidiary, by buying a foreign company, by shipping components for local assembly, by licensing someone to make your products for you, or selling your know-how to a local company so that it can both manufacture and sell. The money you receive from the local licensee then increases the total invisible earnings of the country and of your own company.

The growth in invisible earnings has been largely unrecognized until recently, partly because these earnings were never officially included in Britain's balance of payments figures, and partly because there had been a drop in these earnings as foreign countries took over assets owned by British companies. But now the money earned from "invisibles" is growing fast – it has probably already reached £500 million a year – and it is held that licensing and know-how arrangements are responsible for about one-fifth of this total. In fact, without earnings from invisibles our balance of payments would be somewhat precarious.

Licenses and know-how

Before going on to examine how your company may be able to profit from an asset it may not know it has, let me explain that granting a company overseas a licence to manufacture your product locally, and selling your know-how are not quite the same thing, although many people use the two terms somewhat indiscriminately.

Licensing is strictly speaking granting someone permission to do something which would otherwise be an "actionable wrong". It means in effect that the licensor allows the licensee to carry out the patented method of manufacture for a specified length of time. And in theory the licensor gives the licensee the technical information to enable the process to be used. As a patent specification is a public document, then if the licensee breaks the agreement, for example by failing to pay, the licence can be revoked.

On the other hand, know-how means in effect technical knowledge. When granting the right to use know-how one makes available, not only the knowledge but also the practical experience gained from the application of the knowledge. But it is not so easy to take effective action against anyone who breaks a know-how agreement because one cannot withdraw knowledge or information once it has has been supplied. Hence know-how is often sold on a one-off basis, for a once-only cash payment.

The main point is that it is better to treat the provision of know-how on a different basis from the grant of the patent licence itself. Indeed, there may be a case, if both are to be sold for making two separate arrangements. But against this, the success of any grant of a licence to manufacture and sell locally, and the provision of know-how will rest on a considerable degree of confidence between the two parties, so that as long as this distinction is remembered, in practice it can often be ignored.

What do you have to sell?

Any manufacturer who is reading this article will realize that he has probably something to sell in this field of licensing. He is likely to have one or more patents on his products. He may only have patent applications, but even these are saleable. It is possible that a company has something special to sell in the way of manufacturing or application techniques. Maybe the product has an edge over the competition in its design or performance. Perhaps the raw materials are blended or used in an unusual way. Somewhere, any successful company has something to sell in relation to the manufacture or sale of a product or process, because it is that which keeps it competitive in this country. After all, even a trade mark is a very saleable proposition if it is sufficiently well known.

In other words, you may well be sitting on a hidden asset which you do not realize you can sell at a profit. And remember that in addition to selling a licence to manufacture and exploit a product locally, you may also be able to sell other licences for the components and raw materials to enable exploitation of the main licence. This is particularly true in East European markets where licensees usually want to import both the plant and the raw materials to go with it.

Moreover, you will appreciate that this is one way a small or medium-sized company can increase its earnings from overseas without having to invest in a new factory. It can enter markets hitherto closed to it, without having to step up production to meet the demand, and without having to spend vast sums of money on hiring more people

And remember that virtually all the countries in the world, including those in Eastern Europe, adhere to the Paris International Convention for the Protection of Industrial Property, probably one of the most important treaties in the field of industrial property ever to be signed. Briefly, this convention means that if a patent is applied for in one country, the application date can be used as if applications had been made in any other Convention country, provided an application is made during the twelve months following the original application date.

What is required overseas

While you are wondering what in fact your company has to offer in this way, it will be helpful to look at some examples of the kind of things those markets that are protected by high tariffs and quotas are looking for.

Starting with the major Latin American markets such as Brazil, the Argentine, Mexico and so on, many are building their own ships, but they require the technology and the technical equipment to go into the hulls of these ships. They are looking for help in the petro-chemical field, and technical assistance in building hospitals, airfields, underground systems, and extending their ports and harbours.

Move over to Europe and take a look at the Portuguese. They need to mechanize their agriculture. They want to produce more refrigeration and air-conditioning equipment. Many people who visit Portugal for a holiday do not realize that around Oporto there has grown up quite an efficient light engineering industry, which is always looking for things to make. And next door to Portugal is Spain, which requires know-how in her steel industry, paper mills, and chemical plants. Spain needs a whole host of consumer durables, but can afford to import but few of them, so needs help to make them locally.

To the east is Turkey which has received more aid from Britain than we have given to any other country. It is being spent on anything that will develop local industry, and thus satisfy a demand for consumer goods that cannot be met from outside, because of Turkey's severe balance of payments problem.

Step behind the Iron Curtain where the demand for know-how and technical help is insatiable. Chemical and rubber plants are being built. All forms of transportation are being developed. Data processing is being used continually in industry. Anyone who has seen the queues at a Moscow department store will know of the enormous demand for consumer products, which can only be satisfied by stepping up local production facilities. Many markets in Africa and the Far East are also anxious to lessen their dependence on imported goods, and make locally many products they formerly imported.

In addition, remember that if a product is manufactured locally, then its price is probably likely to be less than if it is sent in from outside. And even if there are no customs duties to pay in a free trade area, the saving on transport costs when supplies are delivered from a local factory may result in lower prices.

The competition

But before you go overboard on the whole idea of local licensing, do not run away with the idea that everything will be plain sailing. The competition will be intense, because the French, the Germans, the Japanese, the Americans and the Italians are all trying to sell their expertise. To take one example, Mexico has issued a list of over five hundred "new and necessary industries" it would like to see developed, and that is in addition to the 200 or so already established there. But the queue of salesmen from other countries knocking on the Mexicans' door is never-ending.

Similar conditions exist in other markets, notably in Eastern Europe, where any large project attracts attention from nearly all the major European countries. So you will face competition in selling a license or know-how in exactly the same way as you face competition when you try to sell a product manufactured in this country.

A total export operation

And again, before you get too excited about the possibilities of making money from licensing, you must consider it in relation to your total export effort, and not as a substitute for doing direct exporting. Selling your know-how should be part and parcel of any total exporting operation. You must decide between exporting your product from this country, and licensing people overseas to make and sell it for you. And this will depend on the extent of your exports, the countries to which they go, and the facilities you have for increasing production, or the necessity for limiting it. It will also of course depend on how much people overseas want to manufacture your product under licence, and this in turn will depend on what demand there may be for the end product.

Where do you start?

First you must review the whole of your company's export policy and decide the areas where you may wish to consider licensing. These may be in existing markets or they may be in the markets where you are not already doing business. But it is essential that this study is made so as to pinpoint the areas where you will be happy to consider selling licences to manufacture, and possibly also to sell.

Next you must decide precisely what it is you wish to sell, and the reasons why you wish to sell it. The classic example of licensing is probably Pilkington's Float Glass. Here, the company has something quite new, a process of producing flat glass which was new, and which no one else had. The cost of developing this process had run into millions of pounds, so one way to recoup some of this capital cost was to sell the rights of local manufacture for cash. Another reason in their case was that in many export markets they were already suppliers of a great deal of other types of glass. Had they themselves manufactured the new glass locally they would have antagonized many of their best customers. And in other markets the only way for Pilkingtons to get in behind the import restrictions was to manufacture locally, but under licence.

If the sale of trade marks or patents is involved, then it must be clearly established whether the former have been registered and the latter granted in the markets concerned, how long they are valid and so on. This normally has to be done country by country, although once we join the EEC we shall have the advantage of being able to use their facilities for registering trade marks in about fourteen countries at the same time.

You must next carry out research to establish whether the various markets you have in mind want your product, or whether it will need to be adapted in any way. Probably a great deal of this information will already exist in your export department, but if not, then it must be obtained. It is clearly a waste of time to try selling a licence to manufacture shoes in a market where most people go bare-footed. And you must ensure that this product suitability study is done in depth in each country, because on it will largely depend the amount of money you can expect to make from selling a licence.

None of this should be beyond the capabilities of an efficient export department. If it is, you will need to use an outside consultant to do it for the company. Since this is so often long-term development work, it may pay you to use a consultant if your export department is fully committed on day-to-day export trade.

The fullest use should be made of the facilities of the Department of Trade and Industry, which can provide you with information about the opportunities in each export market. And if you decide to go further they will arrange, through their commercial officers overseas, to put you in touch with likely licensees. When you go to see these, as go you must finally, they will arrange introductions and appointments. Ask your bank to help, because banks are particularly knowledgeable about local companies who can afford to invest in purchasing licences. Go and talk to your local Chamber of Commerce. Some make a small charge for this kind of work, but usually only when it is a question of obtaining names and addresses of likely purchasers overseas.

Get in touch with two useful bodies, the first being the Licensing Executives Society at 11 Charles Second Street, London, SW1. The other is the National Institute of Licensing Practitioners at 69 Cannon Street, London, EC4. The Licensing Executives Society represents the interests of licensing executives in industry. Its members are mostly drawn from the patent, trade mark or licensing departments of larger firms. The National Institute of Licensing Practitioners is the only UK body of professionally qualified licensing practitioners providing independent advice on all licensing matters.

If you are particularly interested in selling licences to Eastern European countries, then two bodies have special sections dealing with this part of the world. One is the CBI at 21 Tothill Street, London, SW1. The other is the London Chamber of Commerce at 69 Cannon Street, EC4. The DTI should also be able to help following its taking over of the responsibilities formerly discharged by the BNEC.

What sort of licensing agreement?

There are so many variations of agreements that it is almost impossible to lay down any standard agreement form, but the way to approach drawing one up is to treat it in the same way that you draw up an agreement with an agent or distributor in an export market.

The main ingredients of an agency agreement cover the parties to the agreement and the purpose of the agreement. Next the territory to be covered must be precisely laid down, and there must be no ambiguity about this – not like the agreement in which one manufacturer signed away his manufacturing rights to a company for 'the southern half of Africa'. No one could agree exactly where the borderline came!

Instead of then specifying the goods to be supplied, you must substitute precise details of what is being sold – that is to say the product or products that may be manufactured under licence, and the information and know-how that will be supplied, either on a one-off or continuing basis. This is usually followed by the basis of remuneration – which is dealt with below – and how this is to be paid. Then there is the duration of the agreement to be considered and its termination terms. Finally it is necessary to specify what arbitration there is to be in the event of a dispute, and the law under which this agreement is made. If you are selling a trade mark as well, remember to specify the goods or products for which it may be used.

This all needs to be contained in a precise written document. East European countries insist on a written document. Other countries do not always insist, but for one's own protection licence and know-how agreements must always be written contracts, and as unambiguous as possible. And above all, the negotiation of such an agreement must be done in the country concerned, not only to ensure that you both know and understand each other, but because you will wish to reassure yourself that the local company has the facilities to exploit the licence to your mutual advantage.

Finally, remember to include in any agreement your wishes about whether the licence can be transferred to a third party. This is seldom allowed, but needless trouble in later years will be avoided if a clause on this point is included.

What you can expect to be paid

The payment you receive obviously depends on the value of the licence to the buyer, but normally you can expect to receive between two and seven per cent on signing the agreement, based on what the licensee can reasonably be expected to make and sell in the first year. Since it may take him time to get going, this is often based on the first 18 months' prospective sales.

You can then expect an annual royalty of the same amount

based on the same calculations. But you should insist on a minimum annual figure, if only because this will prevent anyone buying up your licence to prevent someone else using it. This could happen, for example, if a licensee wished to keep a competitive product off the market. You may, of course, negotiate a higher annual royalty without any initial downpayment, but in such cases it is usual to ask for the first year's royalty in advance, in exchange for supplying the necessary information to the prospective licensee.

In East European markets, royalties on sales are uncommon, licences usually being bought outright for cash. Where such licences are tied to the supply of raw materials or components, you may be asked to accept payment in instalments, because the licensee may have to exploit the licence before he can find the money to pay for it.

Remember that ECGD will insure you against the risk of non-payment for royalties and down-payments through their 'Special type policies for service contracts'. It is always worth insuring yourself in this way, because once having supplied information you cannot get it back. Hence one covers oneself against the inability of the licensee to pay due to circumstances outside his control, such as unexpected currency restrictions.

Additional benefits of licensing

In addition to the immediate cash benefits a company can expect to obtain from licensing in an export market it cannot afford to develop (Japan is a good example of such a market), there may well be fringe benefits. One of these is of course the supply of raw materials, components and replacement equipment.

An example of how this works is a manufacturer who has produced a new method of rust-proofing cars. He has sold the rights to the process, but he still supplies the sealant. It is, in fact, a condition of the licence that only this sealant may be used when exploiting the licence. In such cases the raw material may be supplied at cost, to keep import duties to a minimum, and the size of the royalty adjusted accordingly.

Other less tangible benefits are many, such as the feedback of ideas in the manufacturing process, the design of the product itself, and developments in its uses. It has been found that local licensees have in many cases hit upon developments that the parent company has not thought of, and one should always build into any agreement a "two-way ideas clause". Equally it is necessary to ensure that modifications are not made to the process locally without the consent of the licensor.

Some licensing agreements are now based on what are called "reverse investment options", which means that royalties are converted into shares in the licensee's company. This means you start to build up a joint venture in the market with a local company. This option is also used where royalties cannot be repatriated at the present time, but where a long term investment in that country seems a sound proposition.

It will have been obvious that it is impossible to lay down any hard and fast rules about the form any local licensing agreement should take, because this must vary with the product, the trade, and the local conditions. But within this broad framework any company should be able to work out a licensing agreement most suitable for that company.

But let me stress that this is an additional benefit to a company and should never be looked at purely as an alternative to direct exporting. It must involve a complete study of the company's total export policy, which is generally best done by outside consultants who can be objective and who are able to draw a balance between these two forms of earning money from overseas markets.

Nobody will make a fortune out of local licensing, but it can provide a useful contribution to a company's revenue, and in particular to the costs of research and development. And of course it will increase the value of your trade marks and company reputation by widening the areas in the world in which you operate. But to make money you must be prepared to spend heavily on that initial research, because on it will depend the price you get for your licence.

6

A NEW LOOK AT THE
LIFE CYCLE OF PRODUCTS

Martin Van Mesdag, a distinguished Dutch consultant, writes that the life cycle concept has much unexploited potential.

No marketing man would ever admit to being ignorant of the "Product Life Cycle Concept". Indeed, the idea of attributing behavioural characteristics to inanimate objects and then comparing them to parallel characteristics in living things is something that fascinates human beings from early childhood – in fact particularly in early childhood. Knowledge about the product life cycle concept for many people – some marketing men included – goes just about this far: the life of a product in a market is likened to the life of a human being.

It is the purpose of this article to qualify this view and to add one or two thoughts which might help to elevate the product life cycle concept from its present status of quaint gimmick to that of a useful management tool. The reason for encouraging the reader to revisit the product life cycle is a belief in its potential as an aid to marketing planning. The concept appears to encompass such a wide range of measurable phenomena that much more exploitation seems possible. Here, if anywhere in marketing, we have an under-utilized opportunity to apply masses of historical data to the building of models for use in planning. To quote Harry Henry: "If rootlessly you have no knowledge of the past, and no understanding that it matters, then inevitably you are at the mercy of every frolic wind . . . ."[1]

[1] Harry Henry: *Perspectives in Management, Marketing and Research* (1971).

Falseness of the human analogy

The first thing to do is to discourage the idea that the life cycle concept depends on endless parallels between living beings and inanimate objects. To begin with, in as much as there could be discussion about the powers that influence the origin and lives of living beings, no such discussion is relevant in the case of products: they are man-made and the "lives" of products are wholly and entirely dependent upon the actions and attitudes of human beings. Secondly, the purpose in life of a living being is a matter for debate. There is no uncertainty about the purpose in life of a product: it is created to generate a profit.

Only two generalizations can be made about the useful (i.e. profitable) life of products in markets:

1. The life-span of all products is continually decreasing. (Another contrast with what is happening to human beings!)

2. Products from areas characterized by a high rate of technological development, fashion products and discretionary-choice-type products have relatively short lives; commodity-type products have relatively long lives.

The hula-hoop was conceived and born, lived its extravagant and highly cosmopolitan life, aged and died, all in about six months. Coal, as a source of power, has been with us a few hundred years, and looks like being around for a while yet.

In the expression "product life cycle" the term "product" means all the products with a particular set of characteristics that appear within the market confines under discussion. In other words, I do not refer to one manufacturer's particular product or brand, but to the total offering of a given product by him and his competitors.

Strategic implications

The ultimate significance of the life cycle concept is, hopefully, that it provides the marketer with an additional tool with which to sustain the future profitability of his business. Costly mistakes have been made in marketing, owing to failure to recognise symptoms, which an insight into the product life cycle concept would have gone a long way to avoid.

The strategic significance of the product life cycle concept to the marketer is threefold:

1. It provides an insight into the likely performance of products in the near future, furnishing useful pointers for desirable changes in almost every aspect of its marketing mix

2. It acts as an early warning system for taking innovative measures to extend a product's useful (i.e. profitable) life.

3. It shows when new products need to be developed to fill impending gaps in corporate profit objectives.

The product life cycle theory

The following is a brief outline of the Product Life Cycle theory.[1]

It is convenient to break down a product's life into phases and to give a description of the symptoms occurring in each (see chart on page 66).

Development

The first phase describes what happens before anything appears on the market. Time, effort and money are spent on an idea or a concept, sometimes in substantial quantities. There is a high probability that this investment will not be recouped from the product that results from all this back room work. The product may miscarry. However, for the product that is successfully launched, this back-room work will be highly significant, since it determines to a large measure the amount of time needed for competitors to enter the market on a me-too basis. Obviously, the higher the investment needed to enter the market and the more technically complex the product, the greater the lead over competition is likely to be. However, the greater the novelty of the product (and this need have no relation to the investment that went into its development), the longer it tends to take to penetrate the market.

[1] This description is taken from a paper delivered by the author at the 1970 Esomar Congress.

Pioneering

The introductory phase, from the moment the product first appears on the market, is one of slow growth and low volume. Unless the originator deliberately chooses to play it alone for as long as possible, unit price is high. Penetration is low and confined to what Prescott called the "early adopters",[1] the quite deliberate, innovative consumers. The distribution channel handling the product may at this stage have been chosen on a "first come, first served" basis, rather than with any calculated aim for volume potential. The advertising and promotion expenditure is very high on a per unit basis, advertising being created to foster awareness of the product's existence. There are few or no competitors. The number of varieties in which the product is offered is very limited; in fact, experiments are being done repeatedly in order to get the bugs out of the product and to achieve acceptance by the limited circle of early adopters. Sales of the product may remain limited to this category of users for years, heavily taxing the originator's financial resources.

Rapid Growth

Then, sometimes fairly suddenly, sales begin to accelerate. Quite frequently the early adopters, who are rather deliberate users, cause the use of the product to be something of a status symbol and the resistance to change in habits of other consumers begins to break down. Even before imitative competition starts the originating company may have to lower prices to enhance penetration of the product into broader user categories. Rapidly increasing volume begins to enable the originating company to realise attractive margins of profit; in fact, during this stage unit profit tends to reach its maximum as increased volume begins to enable economy of scale characteristics to be established. The properties of the product have become stabilised. Total advertising and promotion expenditure rise rapidly during this phase, although it decreases on a per unit basis. Emphasis will shift from creating awareness towards the achievement of a maximum sampling effect.

[1] Raymond Prescott: "Law of Growth in Forecasting Demand," *Journal of the American Statistical Assn.* (1922).

Depending on the amount of protection (through patents or sophisticated technology, for instance) the originating company has obtained, the rapid growth in volume and the high profitability will form a pressing invitation to imitative competition. Penetration in the original distribution channel tends to become complete towards the end of this phase; price competition by that time has started to bring down unit price and unit profit with it. Total profits may continue to grow a little way into the next phase. With the rapid increase in the number of competitors, however, maximum profitability for any of the early entrants in the competitive race is likely to have been reached and passed during this phase. The sales curve is concave throughout this phase. Level or declining volume growth rates mark the beginning of the next phase.

Maturity

During this phase the competitive jockeying for position starts in earnest. Competition, like the law of the jungle, sifts out the weaker brands. Whilst product differentiation for the basic product diminishes, proliferation of types, sizes, colours, flavours and models starts. Full penetration of the consumer market is achieved, and for durables replacement sales are gaining in importance. Unit prices come down sharply in the early stages of this phase, levelling out towards the end of it.

Market shares of the big brands tend to grow as the cost of market entry now increases relative to the per unit margins available. New distribution channels are opened, adding to the diffusion of product ranges carried by the various "branches" of the retail trade. Per unit rates of advertising and sales promotion will drop further, as will total expenditures for the product category as a whole towards the end of this phase. Promotional themes show a strong trend to brand claims: dealer promotions gain in relative importance and so does merchandising. New entries into the market are few near the end of this phase; in fact, fewer competitors remain than at the beginning. When sales growth rates dwindle to nothing, this denotes the final phase.

Decline

Customers are bored. The product is no longer exciting. In the case of durables the market is made up almost entirely of replacement sales. Consumables are fighting a losing battle against more up-to-date substitutes, or are simply failing to reach younger consumers. The number of competitors decreases. The drop-outs not infrequently mark their death-rattle by severe price cutting. Competition amongst the survivors does the rest to bring about a substantial drop in unit prices, and, thereby in total market revenue. Total profitability for the product category falls sharply, and may disappear altogether. The battle for market shares continues in both existing and in yet further new distribution channels. Advertising expenditure drops to very low levels and so, eventually, does promotional expenditure. The remaining competitors make further attempts at segmentation.

Eventually, manufacturers, recovering their variable cost and only part of their fixed cost, drop the product line or go out of business. Rather unpromising defensive mergers sometimes occur. Very occasionally one or two manufacturers settle in the remaining ruins to lead a spartan but not necessarily unhealthy life. Somebody still makes braces and sock suspenders and pocket watches and cocoa powder and pipe tobacco. More rarely still, such ardent hangers-on may be lucky: candles have been given a new lease of life (they are no longer used for lighting, but for creating an atmosphere of semi-darkness) quite apart from artificial booms caused by power cuts. Enamel kitchen-ware and cast iron stoves are making a come-back in the nostalgia market.

Isolating distorting influences

It is clear that any significance to be derived from the product life cycle concept emanates from trends, i.e. the product's marketing "behaviour" related to time. Before looking at these in a little more detail it is necessary to point to influences that can distort the pretty picture of trends in the Product Life Cycle diagram.

There are two kinds of influences. Both must be recognized, foreseen and isolated. The first kind of influence is imposed from

Simplified characterization of product behaviour

	Introduction	Rapid growth	Maturity	Decline
Market penetration	low, early adopters	sharp increase	reaches peak	decreasing
Distribution	low, usually single "branch"	sharp increase, mainly single "branch"	saturation in original channel, new types of outlets discovered	remains high initially, but attrition follows
Consumer typology	homogeneous group of deliberate users	increasingly heterogeneous, some turnover, segmentation starting	segmentation reaches peak, high turnover	elderly and traditional
First/replacement/ second unit	first	first, replacement starting	replacement and second unit gaining on first unit	replacement mainly, some second unit
Differentiation	considerable	reducing	low	low
Proliferation	none	beginning	reaches peak	decreasing
Unit price	high	sharp drop	levelling	further drop
Pricing characteristics	differentiation	some differentiation and fluctuation	very stable	defensive, protection sought
Number of brands	one or few	rapid increase	few new entries, sifting	rapidly decreasing
Share of brand leaders	unstable	fluctuations	increasing	increasing
Incidence of private labelling	none	rapid increase	further increase to levelling out	rapid decrease
Share of private labels	none	building up	increasing, reaches peak	dropping rapidly
Total advertising and promotion expenditure	high per unit	decreasing per unit, rapid increase in total	per unit fairly stable, total still increasing but levelling later	sharp decrease
Ratio advertising to promotion	high	decreasing gradually	further decrease	decreasing to little or nothing
Advertising and promotion theme	aimed at product awareness and applications	aimed at strong sampling effect	brand claims, dealer promotions	price promotions, revival attempts

the outside, i.e. outside the relationship between the suppliers and their market. Such influences can be lasting changes in prices of raw materials, economic or political upheavals, the imposition of government-measures, legislation or changes in taxation. The distorting effect of increases in the duty on tobacco can be very clearly recognized when plotting amounts of tobacco used in cigarettes consumed in the UK, to quote one obvious example.

The second kind of distorting influence is "internal": it is very much part of the relationship between suppliers and their market. It is the influence on product life cycles of innovation in a product or in other aspects of its marketing mix, or innovation through substitution of that product by a new product which may come from a new source.

There is a cause-and-effect characteristic about innovation in relation to product life cycles. Earlier, innovation was mentioned as a strategic measure, the need for which can be discovered by using the product life cycle concept. But innovation is itself one of the influences that can distort a product life pattern. It all depends whose point of view you are taking, of course; that of the innovator or that of the suppliers of a product being replaced.

The crucial thing to remember is that very few products get sick or die because their suppliers decide to lower quality or increase price unduly – many products, in fact, get better and/or cheaper as time passes. Most products age and die because other products, often technologically unrelated, come along which are more convenient, better looking, more varied, that save time, are safer, or taste better. From the point of view of the original suppliers of a product in a market such "replacement innovation" can be so sweeping as to distort the life cycle pattern of the original product.

Concept not only applicable to products

The product life cycle concept has been used in forecasting things like home-ownership of certain durables, the number of retail stores with self-service facilities and the profitability of door-to-door selling. Neither is the use of the concept confined to consumer products. M. T. Cunningham[1] shows interesting examples of its use for industrial products.

Strategic implications

The following are a few examples of the strategic implications of all this.

(a) When an originator company begins to experience accelerating sales growth of its new product (or, alternatively, when success is indicated in a test marketing situation), an insight into the life cycle theory makes it imperative that a pricing strategy is determined. Is the company going to fend off competitive entries by a low price level for its product in an attempt to maintain a maximum market share for as long as possible? Or, alternatively, will it aim for a high price level, thus inviting competitive entries and stimulating the total growth rate for the product group as a whole?

(b) On the assumption that a company can assess the lead time for product improvements, or for new product introductions, the use of the life cycle concept can help to plan innovations by acting as an early warning system for declining profits on existing products.

(c) Some of the defensive mergers between companies with all of their products in the maturity and decline phases would not occur if the prospective partners were fully aware of the stage of life of the other's products. Governments might not give investment grants or other forms of aid to industries if they knew that by so doing they were merely prolonging an unfortunate obsolescence.

Factors and implications

If the product life cycle concept, as is sometimes suggested, merely referred to sales volume, profits and unit price, then its

[1] M. T. Cunningham: "The application of product life cycles to corporate strategy: some research findings," *British Journal of Marketing*, 1969.

practical use would be questionable indeed. There are, as I have already indicated, quite a number of other characteristics in the "behaviour" of products in markets which show significant trends.

If these other characteristics can be identified and if they can be measured then all we need to learn is how to correlate those trends and what inference can be drawn as to the expected profitability of the product under study. The state of the art has not evolved this far yet. Although quite a lot of data are collected relative to product's performance and behaviour in the market-place, very little has been done to construct models to act as profit forecasting tools.

The factors which, I believe, are characteristic of the stage of life products are in, and which, consequently, are potential indicators of a product's profit performance are:

(a) Market penetration

Penetration is the ratio of regular buyers to the number of people to whom the product is of potential interest. For most products, there is little problem in measuring penetration. There are various continuous or repetitive marketing research services that measure penetration in any degree of detail required.

(b) Distribution

Distribution is the ratio of the number of stores selling the product to those that could be potentially handling it.

There is no problem in finding out how many grocers or garages carry item X or item Y out of all grocers or all garages respectively. The problem is to determine how many stores from each trade channel are *potential* sellers of the product. The complexity of this problem increases every day (as anyone who realizes how a few years back grocers did not sell stockings, garden centres did not sell chocolates and garages did not sell snacks, will appreciate).

(c) Consumer typology

Is there one group of people that tends to buy the product and another that does not, and, if so, what are the attitudes towards the product of each group? It is changes in these attitudes that are relevant to our purpose. I would note here that I do not believe in attempts that have been made from time to time to identify 'early adopters' as such. I do not believe such people as universal "early adopters" for all types of products exist. Whereas there may be a category of people who rarely display a pioneer attitude towards new products of any kind, most consumers will be early to buy new products in some cases and slow to adopt them in others.

(d) Ratio of first to replacement purchases, and incidence of second unit (durables)

The usefulness for our purpose is obvious, its measurement no problem. It is quite possible that the development of the market for second (or subsequent) items in the household will prove to be, to the alert life-cyclist, quite a new market in the marketing sense (think of radios and motor cars), and should be treated as such.

(e) Product proliferation

The number of varieties, sizes, applications, (optional) extras, colours, flavours, combinations – in short the proliferation in which a product is offered usually increases in all but the last stages of its life. Monitoring this development is an easy matter.

(f) Product differentiation

This must not be confused with the previous symptom, product proliferation. Product differentiation refers to the qualitative and technological differences between products as offered by the various competing suppliers. Early on in the life of products differences tend to be greater than subsequently. Suppliers are experimenting with formulae and processes, establishing the basic physical properties of the product.

Motor cars offer an interesting illustration of both the proliferation and the differentiation symptoms: proliferation of models, colours, extras, power-packs, today is greater then ever. Differentiation (say, between manufacturer A's 4-cylinder family saloon and manufacturer B's 4-cylinder family saloon) has been reduced substantially compared with say, 40 years ago. In most cases changes in the degree of differentiation (for that is what is relevant in our context) are not difficult to establish.

(g) Number of competing brands

The number of competing brands, and increase or decreases in that number, changes in the "cost of entry" into the market, the pattern of market shares and the change in the (combined) share of the market leader(s), all relate to the stage in the relevant product's life.

Similarly the incidence of private labelling the growth and, later, the drop in combined private label market share should be taken into consideration. Aggregate private label share as such does not indicate anything about the stage a product's life has reached.[1] Measurement of these characteristics using conventional methods, should be no problem.

(h) Advertising and sales promotion

The proportion of expenditure on theme advertising, on merchandising on sales promotion, and the proportion of the total budget spent on activities to obtain product sampling tell us something about the stage in the product's life cycle, and so does the total expenditure for advertising and sales promotion as well as total expenditure per unit of sale.

The general adoption of advertising platforms explaining product properties or applications is clearly indicative of the introductory or early growth phase of a product, just as the battle of competitive claims heralds maturity. The decline phase, in as much as there are any suppliers left with enough courage and money, may show revival type advertising.

It is in these last areas, in particular, that careful analysis of what goes on over time can help in foreseeing what changes in the mix and the usage of marketing tools is likely to be needed in the near future. Fortunately for quite a number of products there are good sources of advertising expenditure data. This is not normally

[1] See first issue of Audits of Great Britain Limited's *Audit* Magazine (1971).

the case for "below-the-line" expenditure, where a proper assessment can be quite tricky.

(i) Price fluctuation

Unit prices will tend to come down fairly sharply during the introductory and early growth stages, levelling out as growth continues and early maturity is reached. A further sharp drop during late maturity and early decline is quite possible. In addition to this general trend, unit price fluctuations can occur during the early growth stage. During the introductory and early growth phases quite substantial unit price differentiation is very likely to occur. Observation of these phenomena should be simple.

I am not at all sure that the above is anything like a complete inventory of symptoms that surround the lives of products in markets. They are only the ones that I (and a few others) have recognized. Put down in a very rough and very generalized table they are as shown in the table on page 66.

Conclusion

In what I have termed the symptoms that signify the stages of a product's life in the market there is much that can be measured and evaluated. A lot is already being measured in the case of many products. There are a few facets that defy today's research technology, but there is hope for the future. Already, therefore, there is a lot of building material for the construction of product life cycle models. This ought to constitute a challenge to information managers, especially in companies that need to rely heavily on innovative expansion.

The main areas in which development and experimentation should be undertaken are:

1. The "purification" of product life cycle data by recognizing, isolating and evaluating external and internal distorting influences.

2. The assembly and correlation of data about the symptoms in the life cycles of products and the establishment of inference patterns for their future behaviour, and thus for profitability.

Any additional tool that helps to increase the reliability of profit predictions, and, consequently, pinpoints future profitability gaps, has merit for the marketing strategist, This is increasingly true, since we are living with decreasing average product life spans, and with increasing cost of entry expenditure both in absolute terms and in terms of cost per £ of product revenue.

7
MARKETING:
MAKING THE CONCEPT REAL

How do you convert a company from product orientation to market orientation? That is the question put to Theodore Levitt by Michael Rines, Marketing's Editor, in an interview at Harvard University. Levitt is Professor of Business Administration at Harvard's Business School and is one of the world's leading authorities on marketing.

MR. I'd like to put the problem to you of the chief executive who has been on a course and has swallowed the marketing concept whole. Now he has returned to his company – his production-orientated company – and he wants to convert it to a market-orientated company. How should he do it?

TL. It seems to me that the important thing to recognize with orientation is that, because you're dealing with an organization, there's a great deal to be said for institutionalizing.

MR. Could you explain that?

TL. By "Institutionalizing" I mean orientation change requires its being reflected in specific kinds of action requirements. It's simply not enough to get people to understand and be eager to think in marketing terms, and then hope that things will happen; it's got to be bureaucratized. And the way to get it bureaucratized is to put into it what I would call the Business Plan. I have become increasingly persuaded that that's the way to do it; not to try to create what are called Marketing Plans, but to put it into the Business Plan. The reason for that is that if you put it into the Marketing Plan you are making an assumption that you are doing something different than what ordinarily ought to be done.

Ordinarily, everyone will agree to the necessity of some sort of business plan on an annual basis, even if only to the extent that people develop rudimentary budgets for the following year, or rudimentary projections from which you make certain judgements about production capacity and manpower, working capital, etc.

Everybody does that in some form or another, some more elaborately than others. So put the marketing orientation into that Business Plan. It has the particular virtue of not presuming to create something separate like a marketing plan, and to this extent it reduces some of the resistance in the organisation that you may get. It facilitates the rejuvenating process because it is part of a planning device that is already being employed. Then, when the Business Plan is being discussed, it is possible to introduce market orientation by a questioning process.

If the plan says "We shall do X volume of business next year", then the marketing orientation would ask – "Why?" The answer might be "The population is growing at 3 per cent, that's why we're going to get more". Then it should be pointed out that what such an objective means is "We're going to retain the same market share as we did last year, split up equally". There is an easy enough question to ask on that – "Why are we saying that?" Are we saying competitors are not going to do something new? That customers don't require anything different, that we couldn't do better? And we begin to ask questions that require a focus on the market place.

MR. So basically what you're doing is to make the people involved talk themselves into a market orientation by asking them questions to which *they* find answers?

TL. That's right. And the chief executive has that obligation. He has the obligation not to say didactically "We're going to be marketing orientated now," but to ask those kinds of questions which will result in that kind of plan.

But there is another problem. An organization that is not accustomed to detailed planning has to learn to do it. The worst thing that can be done in my experience is to try to develop a planning mechanism which is more sophisticated than the state of the organisation's capability, or inclination. It's trying to make the organization accept a Rolls-Royce when it doesn't yet know how to drive a Ford. Most people are incapable of this sort of rapid development.

MR. Do you think that alongside this process of making people ask and answer questions there's any case for sending executives on formal marketing courses?

TL. Yes, there is more than one route to market orientation. Sending managers out to the right kind of programme is very, very, helpful, particularly if the programmes provide an opportunity to learn what other firms are doing, not just what some professor like myself might say ought to be done. A realisation of what is being done effectively by others legitimises the marketing concept; it shows one is not alone; it's just like industrial purchasing – if somebody wants to sell you a computer you ask, "Well who else has one; who's done it?"

MR. But because achieving marketing orientation is so much a matter of attitude, it must necessarily be difficult to teach. Do you think that in some cases you would have to get rid of people who just didn't have the flexibility of mind to adapt to the new approach?

TL. That is conceivable. In fact, what we are saying is that the marketing attitude is not a subject one teaches; it's a subject that one learns. In my experience, most people can learn. It's after all nothing very complicated, but attitudes are not as easily changed as shoes. And one of the reasons I favour using the business plan is that it is a way of creating change which in effect turns out to be an attitude change, but where there is no attempt to manage people's attitudes. And business men are very responsive to this.

Anybody who has reached a reasonable level of achievement in an organization where he has grown by his own merits, as opposed to having gone in at that level, knows something about managing change. He's got some skill, and so he's not that incapable of changing. For example, if you ask a man questions about the plan for next year – "How could we do it better? Do we have to sell harder? Sell what harder? This present product? Is there any chance of changing it – the price, the package, the channels of distribution? Who are our competitors?" – you set a dialogue in motion which is a challenge for any reasonable man. And then when you require that something be stipulated on paper regarding the competitive situation, regarding the product plusses and minuses compared with other products, and regarding how you price, regarding how well you did in the north of England as opposed to the south; or France as opposed to Germany, it's inconceivable that a reasonable person who has achieved some rank and position wouldn't in time begin to think about it. He may constantly have to be reinforced, of course.

MR. What we've been talking about so far has been how to change the attitudes of those who are in the marketing area and in a fairly senior position. If we can solve that problem, does the rest follow? It is said that market orientation must be spread right through the company, right through to the shop floor. Will that necessarily follow on?

TL. No, it won't follow on, and in my book *The Marketing Mode*, I've got a few chapters that address themselves to that question. I make the argument that there are very obvious limits to the marketing concept and we recognise them organizationally. Organizationally, for example, the head of manufacturing is an advocate of manufacturing efficiency. He will always argue for long production runs. The marketing man with 100 per cent market orientation will argue usually for the shortest possible production run because he will say there are 49 different consumer categories out there and we want a different product for each one. Well, a different product for each one means the production runs are so short that the cost will go up tremendously. So you have organizational advocates – manufacturing, and personnel, and finance and so on. And you *want* them to advocate a different position. The chief executive in a way orchestrates the differences. In the process of orchestration, he also develops certain kinds of values – which aspects we're going to push harder or less hard in connection with the requisites of the market place. In so far as it goes all the way down the organization I think it's a very useful notion; that is should permeate an organization so that people are more willing and more responsive to the kinds of things which need to be done in order to serve the customer from the point of view of getting the best rate of return. And that requires again some kind of an effort, even down to how your staff answer the telephone and the kind of letters they write.

MR. And how do you bring this need home to them?

TL. Some of it is pure training, I suspect, but if people understand the reasons for what you are asking them to do, then they are more likely to be responsive than if they don't. A perfect example in the United States in these last two years is what happened to the airline industry when suddenly we had large lay-offs – pilots, stewardesses and agents at the ramps. Some of the major companies like United Airlines and TWA went on a big campaign to explain why this had to be done and that in order to minimize the lay-offs they had to do certain things to attract more customers. The next thing you know you have pilots talking more clearly over their loud speaker systems, and stewardesses being more generous in the nature of their behaviour towards customers.

MR. It's a pity it often has to wait for that kind of thing to happen before the explanations are given.

TL. Yes, and that it has to be so negative. But I think there are ways you can do it positively. For example, if a firm brings out a new package, or starts a new promotion it's bad to have most of the employees find out about it after it comes out. It's probably a good idea to explain why; to take them into the firm's confidence. And lots of people are interested; it gives them a sense of belonging which is so desperately needed.

MR. Perhaps we could now talk about changes in structure. There is so little written about the relationship between organization structure and the market situation. The fashionable thing is to be concerned with the behavioural sciences and what the structure is going to do to the staff, rather than what it's going to do in the market place. What are your views?

TL. Well, I believe first of all in the utility of strong decentralized centres of responsibility, rather than the functional type organization. This means allocating responsibility either on the basis of products or of markets. When you've got one product which goes to many different kinds of market, you generally think in terms of market managers. This is often the practice in industrial companies which may be selling the same product to the construction industry, to utility companies, to oil companies. In such cases it seems to me to make a lot of sense for somebody who understands the market and what's going on to be responsible for each particular market. Then, in the consumer field, we have the brand management system, and it may make sense sometimes even to break this down according to the distribution channels. Whichever method is used it's an opportunity to focus in on specific markets or specific products. It creates responsibilities down the line because you can judge how well a person is doing, and it also creates in the organization many new centres of management development which are not that expensive. This is particularly welcomed among the younger people. More than anything they want responsibility, and although they're interested in remuneration, if they have responsibility in rank that's terribly important for them.

MR. Presumably the further you can take things the more powerful it will be, for instance, if a product manager in an industrial set-up controls his own salesmen?

TL. There are some problems in that, as you know. One of the problems is that in some cases the marketing managers don't have any line authority. There are thus certain ambiguities in their function; they may have a lot of responsibility, but not a great deal of authority and the reason for that is that the salesmen have to call on lots of different channels of distribution and may have more than one product. So the product or brand manager has responsibility for the outcome, but not the authority over the people who do the field selling. His task is to try to negotiate more of their time than some other marketing manager in the same company who has to use the same sales organization.

MR. I always suspect that this must rob the marketing effort of a lot of its impact, and that in many cases it would be worth a little bit of geographical inefficiency in exchange for a bit more drive on the market.

TL. I suspect you're right, and the question is: "What are the trade-offs on that?" I think that's a fairly complicated issue and it has to be settled on a situation by situation basis. But I think the general principle that you've stated here tends to hold.

MR. Staying with this business or organization, if we're talking about reorganizing on the basis of market orientation, where do you start?

TL. I think you start by talking about the task. And for our purposes it seems to me you can define it as to create and hold the customer at some acceptable level of risk and with some presumption regarding desired rate of return – the higher the risks, the higher the rates of return. What are the requisites for getting and holding customers?

You must ask what are the decision-making processes of the critical consuming units and what kind of skills, attitudes and resources must the sales organization have to be successful. It seems to me it all stems from the presumption in the annual plan. The plan may say "Here's the kind of money we're going to spend next year for salesmen", and then you can ask the question, "How do you know you have the right number?" "Are they going to operate differently with certain kinds of customers than with others?" If you're in the packaged goods business, you ask "How different is the operation between the small retail grocery store as opposed to the large chains: what are the differences in the kind of people we have to handle; what are the differences in the kind of packages that you give them? Again, what are we thinking about? In this case we're thinking about the critical decision-making unit as the store. The store is the customer – the consumer is somebody else. In the end you're asking the question of how that particular sector of the organization operates relative to the task, which includes not just your product and what you have, but the competitive situation and so on.

MR. Your point reminds me of an article by D. R. Daniel called "Reorganizing for Results". He was making the point that it's important to identify what he called the "key success factors". He gave a number of examples. For example, a number of years ago an airline put all its passenger services together where they had previously been split apart. It recognized that one aeroplane was the same as another and the only differences were in the services offered on board. Daniel reckoned if you could identify the "key success factor", then you should structure the organization to match.

TL. Yes, I think that's right, but not entirely right. The airlines make a good example, but you might find short and long haul customers entirely different. One carries commuters maybe, the other may carry tourists, so it may not be customer service; it may be route management we should have.

MR. Isn't that really another way of saying that the "key success factors" in different parts of a business may be different; we should split into two businesses perhaps?

TL. Well, that's equivalent to talking about product managers; here you talk about route managers. The thing is how did we get to that difference? We got there primarily by seeing that customer service requisites were very critical in the airline business. But you may also find profitability may vary between say, the London to New York route and the London to Frankfurt route. If you have both under the same management the long haul is likely to get more management attention than the other. So there are strong reasons in favour of having different centres of marketing responsibility.

MR. Otherwise one will become neglected?

TL. Sure. But I want to go back to what you said about putting things together like passenger services. Let us assume a situation different from the airline situation. It's still a problem of putting a lot of things together, and the bigger the unit the more inflexible it tends to become. So again there is some presumption in favour of fragmentation into smaller units. Where you come out in that particular situation I don't know. In some circumstances, of course, there is some virtue in centralization and consolidation and the same result as fragmentation can be achieved by frequent changes in the management of the group.

MR. What about some of the new types of structure, like matrix structures and so on. Are these good ways of introducing a better market orientation?

TL. Well, a product manager/brand manager structure is a matrix structure. You've got a brand manager in charge of Birds Custard. He has no authority over the manufacturing of the custard. The one thing we know about the brand manager structure is that upon first introduction it doesn't work. The second thing we know is that it's full of enormous agonies and stress and recrimination. The third thing we know is that where the system has been operating for some length of time it does work. Why is it that when newly introduced it doesn't work very well, and is full of this recrimination and struggle and bitterness and agnosticism and failure, where in many other places where it has been operating for a long time, it operates very well? I think it's precisely because of the complications inherent in a matrix system – not just the change, but the system itself. It is a system distinguished by its "cultural" difference from the functional system. The functional system is strictly vertical. A man is in charge of everything that affects his task. The brand management system is horizontal. A man is in charge of very little that affects his task. So what you're talking about is different cultures, not just different structures. The matrix structure requires a great deal of consultation and negotiation between people inside an organization where there's a presumption of common purpose which is the creation and keeping of customers at a desired rate of profit. The functional structure is highly departmentalized and autonomous, with the presumption that you sell like hell, or you make it as cheap as hell, or you use as little capital as possible. The change from one structure to the other is significant for the difference it implies in the process by which things will be done for the new culture that's introduced. Moving from one to the other is like moving to a different country.

MR. How do you overcome this difficulty?

TL. I don't think you overcome it; I think you learn to baby it along. You pat it on the head; it needs a lot of love, you change its diaper frequently, you give it a lot of rich food, and you're very forgiving and exercise a lot of patience. But there must be no giving up the ideal; it takes time. And you don't try, as I say, to get people to drive a Rolls-Royce the first day. You do a little bit and a little bit and a little bit. The plan must start simple; it can become more complicated as people get more used to it.

MR. Do you think that involving people in writing their own job descriptions in this new kind of structure is a useful way of getting them to understand what you are at, and indeed of coaching them? Or do you think writing job descriptions is wasteful?

TL. I don't know. If you ask somebody to write a job description he'll find a book and write one. The major problem is that it becomes a fetish which passes for the reality. People don't know what their jobs are until they learn to do them in the way in which you'd like to have them done, or the task dictates it should be done once one is involved in doing it. When you have a job description, what you've created is a possibly self-defeating situation. You may end up saying to the manager "You're not doing what you said you would. Why haven't you done it?" I'm not sure that gets you very far. Some people may have had different experiences. My own notion about how learning works is that it works most effectively when people are not aware of the fact that they are learning. For example, if a child has burned his fingers on a stove and you ask him at the end of the day what he has learned, he will tell you "nothing". But he learned a lot; he learned that a hot stove is something to stay away from.

MR. At the same time unless a man knows what he's supposed to be doing, isn't there a danger that he won't do it; and isn't there also a danger that his collegaues won't know what he's supposed to be doing?

TL. I don't know. I suspect I'm a little bit in the minority on this. My feeling is that there are different ways of knowing: that is conscious and sub-conscious ways of knowing, If I gave you a definition of sex would that improve your performance? It's like all the sex books; I'm not sure they don't create more problems than they solve. I think there are some job descriptions that are more acceptable and those are task descriptions for the next year; objectives in a way; things that we need to do; a dozen lines on a sheet of paper; tasks for the year. I prefer those.

MR. In our chief executive's effort to make his company market orientated, what should he do about an R & D department which in production orientated firms tends to be working on what it wants to make, regardless of the market needs? How does he get it working on market orientated lines? Where does he place it in the organization structure?

TL. Where do we fix it in the organization? That's an impossible question to answer. It sometimes appears under manufacturing, sometimes under marketing, sometimes under an executive at top level, but there is no right place. IBM has had it in every place – more than once. R & D is an organization unique in its horizontal as opposed to its vertical tasks. R & D by necessity cuts across marketing, production and finance. It's very horizontal, which involves it in a lot of negotiation. It has to ask Production if it can make it, Marketing if the customer would like it, Finance if the company can afford it.

Of course, the R & D situation must depend very heavily on the position in the market place the company is going to occupy. The company can aim at being a leader in the creation of new products. Or it can say "We'll never have enough money to be a leader, but we're going to be a follower. Instead of trying to be first, we're going to try to be second, the innovative imitator." In that case, instead of recruiting a lot of students with first class honours it takes students who don't have any honours, but who are satisfied to imitate – it costs less too. The fact is that there isn't a company in the world that has enough resources to be successfully first in everything; it's impossible. So a substantial portion of its work is going to have to be imitative. In this world, unfortunately, this doesn't carry a very high cachet: it may be quite profitable however.

Of course, though it depends very much on the industry, even those companies which do a large proportion of R & D spend most on "D" – (development) – which is mostly imitative. They improve products that already exist, figure out ways of making them cheaper and more compact, more interesting, more attractive, more functional or whatever it may be. But when we talk about "more" we have to be sure it means some form of moreness in the market place and not simply moreness in the laboratory; that's the problem. So a large proportion of an organization's effort is necessarily imitative and must reflect what's going on out there in the market place, what people want, what they might be persuaded to buy, what choice they have, what is going to be most effective?

And that question cannot be answered by somebody sitting in a corner and smoking pot, or thinking; thinking sometimes is just not enough; there has to be some sort of exposure to the market place and therefore some sort of effort to create the exposure.

Instead of some of the researchers going to the convention of the National Physical Society, they should perhaps go to conventions of the Women's Gardens Clubs of America, or some other place where there are consumers.

Some companies try to create exposure by having people spend time with the sales organization, talk with the marketing people, read the marketing plans for next year which talk about the competitive situation and why the company is getting killed here and doing well there. But some effort to create exposure to the environment is essential to the overwhelming proportion of people working in the R & D area. I've known companies that have analysed the market for their products at conferences to which they have invited not only their own internal marketing and sales organizations, but also their scientists and engineers. After all, a scientist or engineer in the end is making a judgement about what is going to work in the market place. For instance, if he decides that a more compact hand-held calculating machine is what he ought to work on he is making an assumption about what people will buy. In some cases the assumption is automatically very good, like if you can make some sort of micro circuit for $10 which ordinarily has been selling for $30. That's a good assumption; there's a high degree of probability that it will be effective. But in most cases decisions made by technical people on their own are not effective.

There was an unbelievable case in the US a few years ago. As you know, the big bottleneck with a lot of computers is the printer. So one company created a non-impact printer that was very, very fast, but one of the problems was that it couldn't make multiple copies. The company argued on the basis of some research that speed was so crucial in so many applications that some customers would give up the necessity for multiple copies. So it went ahead, but it didn't have any way to cut the big paper roll when it came out of the machine and there was no collector for it either. You had to bring a laundry basket to catch it in. How was something so obvious overlooked? It's unbelievable that sane, grown men with PhDs should have developed something with no cutter and no catcher. They were so tantalized with the powerful virtues of speed they forgot the minor details – or rather, they didn't forget, they were just unaware. But, by the simple act of putting those guys into a computer room and letting them see what happened, or by holding meetings to talk about customer product attributes, such a mistake could have been avoided.

MR. Can I take you back to the organizational problem? I accept there are all sorts of different places to put R & D, but are there any guidelines you could give our chief executive? Would there be a case for making it in the initial stages directly responsible to himself so that he can be really sure it's working in the right direction?

TL. Yes and no. If you do that, then the R & D department has the authority of the chief executive's office; that is too much. R & D in my judgement, particularly in the development of products, ought to be in a position where it is in a way compelled to elicit the support of all the people whose support it needs, that is Marketing, Finance and Manufacturing. Otherwise, R & D may develop all kinds of fancy things, that Manufacturing say they can't make, it would cost too much, or gets in the way of present production. And then the sales guy has his problem; he says it isn't elaborate enough, over-engineered and priced too high. So there has to be negotiation that will result in agreement in advance, rather than imposition that will subsequently result in resentment.

Different stages in the development of the company may require different things. If you've got a very intractable sort of ancient organization with ancient, strong-willed men in charge, you may at the beginning want to put it in the chief executive's office or into some higher office reporting direct to him, but in any event I don't believe it should go into any of the existing operating departments. I think I would just make it parallel to all the other operations; that's the preferred position in a mature organization.

MR. Distribution is likely to be another area which in a production orientated firm is likely to be neglected, or at least not looked at as a whole. How would you deal with this in your effort to make the whole company market orientated?

TL. That's an interesting question. It's a critical but highly neglected issue. For instance, you may get an optimum manufacturing unit located in Liverpool, but in practice the location of the market could be such that the cost of distribution may be so high that if you looked at distribution and manufacturing costs as a whole you might find you should have two smaller factories, one in Liverpool, for instance, and one in Birmingham. And the situation can change rapidly, for example when a switch is made from packaging in glass bottles to packaging in plastic bottles. The economics of glass bottle manufacturing are such that you need a big plant, but blow-moulding can be done efficiently on relatively small, cheap machines. So that in glass manufacturing you have a central plant and you ship glass to the place where the bottles are filled and then another 500 miles around to the customer When you get the plastic bottles it's entirely different; you can have a blow-moulding plant built onto the end of your production line and change your plant location sums. In so far as channels of distribution are concerned, it's amazing the constant changes that are occurring, perhaps the most important being caused by the mass merchandiser which means larger consuming units, large customers, and that in turn raises the question of direct selling.

MR. How are we going to make sure that distribution gets the attention it ought to have? Is this another case where one might say that distribution must be organisationally all brought under one umbrella and placed in parallel with the production and marketing departments?

TL. I think there is a presumption in favour of its belonging under marketing. You might say it should belong under manufacturing because the warehouse is in the manufacturing department, but the decisions that have to be taken about distribution are really marketing decisions. Packaging decisions are obviously a matter for the marketing department, but so are many other less obvious decisions. In the steel stock-holding business, for instance, delivery is a very critical part of the customer-getting process. So much so that in the case of the very big customer it might be necessary to rent warehousing space next to his plant in order to provide the necessary level of service. Obviously, the marketing department must be closely involved in such a decision.

MR. Isn't there a danger in putting physical distribution under marketing in that it involves skills like labour relations with which marketing people are unfamiliar? I remember one case where it was put in marketing and there were big problems because the marketing people just did not know how to deal with warehousemen and lorry drivers. Don't you think it safer therefore to leave the physical side to the production department?

TL. It is not safe to assume that the production manager knows how to deal with the labour force all that well! What is really required is that the marketing departmental should employ a manager of physical distribution who *does* know how to handle lorry drivers and warehousemen.

MR. It is sometimes argued we should regard distribution and manufacturing as one total system, particularly when computerization has made it possible to program not just to the warehouse, but right to the customer's door. What is your view of this?

TL. There could be something in it; that's just one of many possible courses to success. I think it pays not to try to be too rigid about these things. The chances are that many organizations moving towards market orientation will try and do too much at the beginning. Distribution may be one of the things marketing organization might find it very useful to lose, and let somebody else have it and get its own way in some more important area. I think the importance of any particular organizational problem varies with the nature of the task that we're talking about. However, I think the notion of product and brand management is so important that I would not give way on it in most situations, whereas I think distribution is less important by comparison.

MR. Perhaps we could go on to the location of the market research function. I have the rather heretical idea that one way you really might get better market orientation is if you have, say, something like a chief executive's office and you have the market research function in there instead of in the marketing department. That way you would really stress the importance of market research; it would be a symbol if you like. Secondly, it would demonstrate that you weren't regarding marketing merely as a function but as something that the whole company had to be involved in. Do you think it would work?

TL. I don't favour that. I don't favour it because again you're giving it the power of that office. I think the chief executive ought to be the orchestrator of the corporate purpose. He can coach and teach and create things, but I think he carries enormous risks if he tries to dictate, because he can so easily be sabotaged. I think the action you suggest says "We're going to get that input to marketing whether you like it or not". I think people have got to learn to do it the marketing way and learn to want to do it. Just imagine the researchers up there on the arm of the chief executive. Why, they're going to get so sabotaged by the rest because nobody will want to tell them anything. "They've got the president's ear, and who are they? They're a bunch of staff, who are they to talk about operating problems?" You can imagine the reactions of the line managers. And remember, sabotage is the most common and least recognised of all forms of organizational behaviour.

MR. Which perhaps leads us on to a point on which I know you have strong feelings – the danger of so-called creative people. Perhaps you could say briefly how you see this danger?

TL. The danger is that the managers who call for creativity are going to achieve the opposite of their intention, because it is not creativity that is wanted; it's innovation, and the two are not synonymous. Innovation is not simply thinking of a new idea, it means also taking some action to implement it. The danger of a flood of new ideas generated without indication of how they will work and what the risks are, is that they cause so many diversions that nothing ever gets done. Managers need more than ideas; they need help to translate ideas into results.

MR. That must be a particular danger in the situation we've been talking about, where you're trying to convert an organization to market orientation.

TL. That's why I say you don't want more ideas – just ask the right questions. Force people to write down how they're going to handle every little detail. That detail becomes the business plan and is the basis for evaluating people's effectiveness in the course of the year.

MR. Do you have any final piece of advice to give to our imaginary chief executive?

TL. Yes, we've been talking about how you do things and whenever we talk about how we do things, the presumption is that you can steal out of your knowledge some general principles, and that there is utility in those principles. I think the more general the principle the less the utility. The bigger the theory the worse it is. I think a good moral should be that there comes a time in the life of every business where one has to abandon principle and do what's right.

8

THE PRICING OF
NEW PRODUCTS

André Gabor is a pricing consultant of international repute who has written many papers on pricing problems. He is currently attached to the School of Economic Studies at Leeds University, and to the Consumer Study Group at Nottingham University. He puts forward here a fully practical method for pricing new products. It should, however, be regarded as a reliable tool when used by a good manager, and not as a mechanical process.

It has become such a widespread practice to bolster up the image of established products exposed to strong competition by adding the prefix "new" to the brand name that the term is on the way to changing its meaning to the consumer, especially since at the same time genuine novelties are frequently supported by publicity which emphasizes that in certain other markets the products has long been established in the favour of the discerning customer.

What is a new product?

In his pedantic way, the economist would define a new product as one which has no near substitute at the time when it is placed on the market. This definition is useful in so far as it points at the difference between what is merely a new brand (or a re-vamped old brand) and a genuine novelty.

The distinction can be carried further. New products may be (a) *functionally identical* with those already in the field, like, say, a new cigarette brand, (b) *functionally similar*, as a new synthetic fibre, or

(c) *functionally unique*, that is to say, dissimilar from anything seen heretofore.[1] It is generally taken for granted that since (*a*) and (*b*) have to find their place in established markets, their prices will be more or less determined by the ruling price structures, whereas in the case of (*c*) the pricing decision has to be made almost in a vacuum. Yet, I would venture to say that it is not the functionally unique but the functionally identical product which presents the more intricate pricing problem.

This point will be discussed later, but first let us have a quick look at some of the expressions of expert opinion.

When should price be based on cost?

The literature of new product pricing includes contributions from a number of eminent authors. The views they express show considerable variety, but there is one proposition that none of them disputes. In fact, they all seem to agree that it is the antithesis of a sensible pricing policy to arrive at the price of a new article by taking its unit cost and adding to it a preconceived percentage to cover both marketing expenses and also profits.'

So be it. Yet it is a fact that this is how the price of many a new product is determined even today, and it must also be admitted that there are situations where the costing approach could not be called unreasonable.

Quite apart from the obvious case of government contracts based on the cost-plus principle, there are people who would claim that this form of pricing is the one most likely to lead to success in industrial markets where the purchasing decision is in the hands of experts who know what the product that they have been commissioned to purchase should cost.

Industrial buyers are not, however, superhuman beings and could not possibly be conversant with the technologies and cost factors of more than a fraction of the items they are commissioned

[1] Richard J. Steele, "Pricing and Level of Newness" in *Creative Pricing* (Elizabeth Marting, ed.), 1968, p. 157.

[2] Paul May, "Retail Pricing," *Gazette of the John Lewis Partnership*, October 1959, pp. 791–93.

to purchase. What they can most often find out is the cost at which they could acquire the product from competitive suppliers, and they should also be able to take into account such non-price factors as the reliability or otherwise of the individual manufacturer, his readiness to deal with complaints, etc.

It follows that in such situations the real purpose of a costing study is not so much the determination of the supplier's own cost, but rather the estimation of the lowest price the keenest competitor may be induced to quote. But unit cost is not an unambiguous concept, and even equally qualified cost accountants using the same basic data are likely to arrive at widely different results, unless they have agreed in advance to use identical rules and conventions, especially as regards the mark-up rates to be applied; hence estimates of competitors' cost can seldom, if ever, be regarded as accurate. Furthermore, unit cost is almost invariably heavily dependent on the quantity concerned and the rate of output. Unless these can be predicted with great confidence, a cost-based price is inevitably a shot in the dark.

This is not meant to deny the importance of cost accounting as a tool of business management. I would say, though, that as far as the pricing of new products is concerned, the principal role of costing is to check the acceptability or otherwise of the price that has been found appropriate with the market in view.

Multistage pricing

Professor Oxenfeldt advocates a multi-stage approach to pricing.[1] Like all sound business economists, he has no belief in any mechanical pricing formula and while he agrees that there are many factors to be taken into account, he is critical of those authors who merely list them and then suggest that "judgement" should help in making the correct pricing decision. Oxenfeldt arranges the major elements into six successive stages the sequence of which appears to be the most essential part of his method. These are the stages, in the order in which they should be tackled:

[1] Alfred R. Oxenfeldt, "Multistage Approach to Pricing," *Harvard Business Review*, July/August 1960.

1. Selecting market targets.
2. Choosing a brand image.
3. Composing a marketing mix.
4. Selecting a pricing policy.
5. Determining a pricing strategy.
6. Arriving at a specific price.

It is obvious that Oxenfeldt is not concerned with the pricing of genuine novelties or functionally similar products the existence of which must be due to inventive innovation. His approach is directed at the pricing problem of functionally identical products and it could be said that his system is a specific form of what has been awkwardly termed by another author "backward cost pricing" It means that the cost to be allowed for the production and marketing of a new product is derived from the price which has been decided upon by marketing considerations.

The first step in Oxenfeldt's system is to take account of the company's position, of the competition it will have to face and of the general situation in the market which it intends to enter or in which it endeavours to extend its sales. This leads to the second stage, where the brand image and the image of the company itself call for decisions. He notes that whereas many distributors pride themselves on the adoption of the principle that they are never knowingly undersold, manufacturers generally prefer a quality image and hence do not like to be regarded as being the cheapest in the market.

Next comes the decision concerning the marketing mix. It calls for the allocation of appropriate amounts to advertising and product improvement, the determination of salesmen's commissions and distributor's rebates, decisions concerning the extent of stocks to be held and other provisions to ensure quick delivery, and, finally, the emphasis to be placed on price appeal. It is not easy to see how one could effectively deal with these aspects at a time when all that is known about the product itself is the image which it is intended to create, but it may not be unwise to formulate preliminary decisions at this stage and revise them in the light of further evidence after the product has been developed.

In selecting a pricing policy, Oxenfeldt suggests a strictly competition-oriented approach, including plans for price promotions and for reactions to possible price changes by rivals.

Oxenfeldt admits that the dividing line between this stage and the next, which concerns strategy, is not clear cut, and suggests that the latter term should be reserved for measures dealing with unexpected special situations, such as, for example, government interference or a general slump.

Once all the five preliminary stages have been dealt with, the range of alternative prices from which the choice has to be made will be very much narrowed. The final decision should then be based on comparisons of cost and expected revenues associated with each price.

Oxenfeldt claims that his multistage approach has definite advantages over other, less systematic, pricing procedures, in so far as it demands a long-range view and allows the price decision to be made in stages instead of requiring simultaneous consideration of all the relevant aspects of the situation.

There is no magic formula for pricing and it would be inappropriate to criticise Oxenfeldt for not having invented one. But it seems fair to point out that while his approach is *methodological*, it does not suggest any actual *method* for the evaluation of the significance of the multiplicity of factors involved in a pricing decision.

Pricing in a dynamic setting

Joel Dean's contributions to the study of pricing have received world-wide acclaim.[1] His works throw light on several aspects of new product pricing, but his main concern appears to be the cultivation of a dynamic outlook. Stated in his own precise words, "new products have a protected distinctiveness which is doomed to progressive degeneration from competitive inroads".

[1] Joel Dean, "Pricing Policies for New Products," *Harvard Business Review*, November/December 1950; also, by the same author, *Managerial Economics*, Prentice-Hall Inc, Englewood Cliffs, NJ 1951 (esp. Chapter 7, pp. 397–467); "Pricing a New Product," *The Controller*, April 1965 (reprinted in *Pricing Strategy*, B. Taylor & G. Wills, eds. Staples Press, London 1969).

Unlike Oxenfeldt, whose multi-stage pricing applies only to products which are new to the company but not to the market, Dean is more interested in the pricing problems of genuine novelties. However, as the above quotation shows, he lays special stress on the progressive decay of the initial novelty, which proceeds more or less simultaneously along three time paths.

Technical maturity manifests itself by the decline in product development and increasing standardization among brands and manufacturing processes. *Market maturity* is indicated by increased consumer acceptance; by the spread of the ability to compare brands and the belief that most if not all, brands give satisfactory service. *Competitive maturity* means that price structures and market shares have reached high degrees of stability.

Dean was the first to point out that there are two essentially different pricing policies for pioneering products: "skimming price" and "penetration price". The terms are self-explanatory and have become common usage since Dean first proposed them some twenty years ago.

Generally speaking, skimming price set at at a multiple of the factory door cost appears to be the safer policy in the early stages for several reasons: (1) demand will almost certainly be restricted and not very price-sensitive at the outset; (2) the high starting price is an efficient device for breaking the market up in segments (if successful, the high price may be retained in the top sector and other segments served by lower priced variants produced by the same firm); it will serve as a "refusal price", and the product will not be marketed unless the initial price generously covers the early high cost; (4) flotation costs will be smaller and more easily recovered than in the case of a low price which demands a high volume of sales. Also, it is easy to change from a skimming price to a penetration price any time during the life cycle of a product, whereas it is, for all practical purposes, impossible to switch from a penetration price to a skimming price.

However, a penetration price is indicated if the product is of the kind which either "goes over big" or not at all; where the highest price acceptable even to a small segment of the market would not leave an appropriate margin over the high unit cost of small-scale production; and where the product is exposed to the threat of early competition.

Clearly, if the distinctive novelty of the product is esteemed by the consumers and not subject to quick deterioration, a skimming price policy is indicated, and the absence of obvious benchmarks for the price must be looked upon as an advantage rather than a detriment of the situation.

Distant benchmarks are best avoided. It would have been a great mistake to price the first domestic vacuum cleaner in terms of the savings on brooms, brushes and dustpans, or the first electric shaver in terms of the razor blades displaced. Some authors suggest that the price maker should establish the utility of the product to the potential purchaser and set the price accordingly.[1] Unfortunately, this is an impossible task, except in those cases where the inducement to buy is in fact restricted to the (calculable) cost savings. This sort of situation is much more likely to arise in the industrial field than in the market for consumer's goods.

The outstanding advantage of the skimming price is that there is little harm in setting it initially too high since it can be reduced whenever this appears to be propitious. This can best be illustrated by an example from the tectbook of a Belgian professor of economics. He describes how a cloth manufacturer would find the price of a new line produced in his workshop. He would take the swatches to one of his wholesalers and watch his reactions. If the samples meet with the wholesaler's approval, he would name the highest price he thinks possible, adding that it is merely an estimate since the costing is still in progress. If the merchant thinks this price would be too high, the manufacturer will promise to watch the costing and then go on to the next wholesaler, trying out on him another, slightly lower price. And so on, by the time our manufacturer has seen half a dozen or so of his main customers he will have a fair idea of the price at which his new line would sell and perhaps even the size of the first orders he may expect to obtain. It is of course possible that even though he started out with the

---

[1] See Robert Ferber, "Contribution of Economics to the Study of Consumer Market Behaviour," *Applied Economics*, May 1969, p. 133.

idea of a skimming price, promises of big orders persuaded him to accept a penetration price instead.

It is now plain why it was stated above that the pricing of a genuine novelty is not such a difficult problem as it may seem at the first glance. But where the product in question is functionally identical with those already in existence, the knowledge of the prices of the established brands is not sufficient to locate the most promising price point for the newcomer.

Fortunately, modern market research can offer effective help towards the solution of this problem.

Finding the best price for a new brand

Pre-testing is often used by manufacturers, and there can be little doubt that substantial mistakes can be avoided by ascertaining at an early stage that the basic characteristics of the product are acceptable to a satisfactory proportion of the potential customers. But it is useless to ask consumers for the price they would be prepared to pay regularly for a product with which they are not properly acquainted. They will heavily undervalue it, especially if it is a genuine novelty.

It is better to approach the problem in an entirely different way, using a method developed by Professor C. W. J. Granger and the present author on foundations laid by Professor Jean Stoetzel of the Sorbonne. It was first described in 1965;[1] since then it has become a standard tool of market research which has proved its worth in many different situations. The method is based on the recognition of the fact that price has a double connotation to the consumer: it is a measure of the cost of the product and a powerful indicator of its quality. This does not of course mean that "the higher the price, the greater the attraction of the product" principle will apply throughout, but it does mean that a launching price that is too low

[1] André Gabor & Clive Granger, "The Pricing of New Products," *Scientific Business*, August 1965. Reprinted in the *European Marketing Research* Review, 1966, also in *Price Policies and Practices* (D. F. Mulvihill & S. Paranka, eds.), John Wiley & Sons, New York, 1967, and in *Pricing Strategy* (B. Taylor & G. Wills, eds.), Staples Press, London, 1969. Cf. also "Price as an Indicator of Quality," *Economica*, February 1966.

can just as effectively kill a new brand as a price that is too high.

Research has provided ample confirmation of Professor Stoetzel's tenet that the consumer intending a purchase will approach the market with two limits in mind. His upper limit is the maximum which he is prepared to pay however excellent the product may appear to be and his lower limit is at the point below which he could not trust the quality.

The limits elicited from a representative sample of potential purchasers can be combined to indicate the possibilities of the market. If the same subjects are also asked to state the price they last paid for a similar purchase, the two distributions together will reveal both the realities and the potentialities of the market.

When presented in diagrammatic form, the relationship between the two curves will show whether or not the leading brands are vulnerable to undercutting, and, combined with the appropriate cost forecasts, it will be possible to locate the price which promises to be the most profitable for a new brand.

The brands selling at or around that price will be indicative of the characteristics which the consumer will expect, and with all this information in hand it should be possible to develop both the product and its image accordingly.

The technicalities of the research methods and the theories of consumers' behaviour to which they have led us are described in detail in our previous publications,[1] but I should like to emphasise here that the "buy-responses" will yield the most reliable data. They are obtained by asking a representative sample of subjects questions of this type: "If you went out to buy for yourself (or for your husband) a white nylon shirt, and you saw the kind you were looking for, would you buy it if the price were £2.50?" Affirmative answers are recorded as buy responses to the price concerned, and their proportion will show the percentage of potential purchasers at this price.

Experience has shown that up to eight or nine prices can be put to the same subject. If the number of prices to be examined is

---

[1] See those listed in footnote 6 and also our paper "The Attitude of the Consumer to Price" in *Pricing Strategy* (B. Taylor & G. Wills, eds.), Staples Press, London, 1969, pp. 132–51.

larger than that, the sample will be have to be split into two or more sub-groups. On the other hand, the same subjects can be tested with prices for three or four different products.

Here then is a fully practical method for pricing new products; a method which is a fact-finder rather than a list of aspects which the price maker should take into consideration. All the same, it should be looked upon as a reliable tool and not as a mechanical process which could replace business acumen. It will be a good tool only in the hand of the gifted manager.

9

THE AGENT: YOUR EXTRA ARM

The agent or distributor overseas should be like an extra arm of your sales force. But all too often the arm becomes withered by the lack of proper motivation and control by the UK principal. Sydney Paulden, who has done extensive research in Europe on the subject, explains how the relationship should be handled in order to obtain the best results.

When outside consultants are called in, it usually means the situation is desperate. This was no exception. The British firm's home market had declined and its European sales had remained stagnant in spite of the joyous claims of all competitors that there was a boom in progress over there.

"It's our agents!" This was the management's main explanation for the trouble. "We'd better sack the lot!" This was the management's formula for putting things right.

Probably at least 3,000 British firms would be right in recognizing this thumbnail sketch as a portrait of themselves, but it is based on a particular instance. The consultant tried to discover the grounds for the company's dissatisfaction with its agents. In the end it had to admit that it had no specific targets for each market, no growth plan and very little idea of how its perfromance compared with that of competitors. As the company had left everything to its agents, it had assumed the agents must therefore take full responsibility – a unilateral contract by neglect.

The consultant did some homework on the markets in Europe for the firm's products, worked out some reasonable targets and then personally visited the agents in each territory. He was now able to put questions on the spot about market shares, sales efforts, promotions, frequency of sales calls and so on, and indicate that he could not be fobbed off with replies not founded in fact. As an outsider, he could learn from the agents what their opinions were of the British principal.

This work, carried out over a period of about six months, provided the consultant with more than enough material on which to base his recommendations. He went back to the manufacturer with his survey and report, to be greeted with the words: "Oh, we don't need any changes now. During the past six months our agents have really got going. Business from Europe is coming in at a rate more than double this this time last year." "Yes," said the consultant, "you are now doing one-fifth instead of only one-tenth of the business you should be doing."

A depressingly large section of British exporters imagines that the first step into a European market is to appoint an agent, and then goes on to make the even greater mistake of assuming that it is then the agent's job to control the market. This attitude often stems from a feeling that the firm is supported by the home market and any business from across the Channel is a useful means of topping up. They compare their export performance with their home performance, whereas the truly international market-minded managements compare their performances in foreign markets with their targets for those markets. There is usually no logical reason for foreign business being any particular percentage of home business, unless your only aim is to get a Queen's Award and a knighthood for exporting so many per cent!

The agency profile

Stress has to be laid on the exporter's knowledge of the foreign market, because it is only from a profile of the market that it is possible to draw a profile of the ideal agent for that market. The more that is known of the task, the better it is possible to decide the kind of tools needed for its successful accomplishment.

It is essential, for example, to be specific about the agent's size and financial resources; the location of his HQ and branches; the type and qualifications of his salesmen and/or technicians; the extent of the services he must offer; the type of sales outlets with which he should be most familiar; the desirable warehousing, transport and stockist facilities; the product ranges he is presently handling and the type of products he could not continue to handle because they would be considered competitive.

Although the word "agent" is used somewhat loosely here, the exporter himself would have to define for his own benefit whether the representation would be a "commission agent", or an "exclusive distributor". The former simply receives a percentage on the orders he generates from the exporter. The latter buys and sells on his own account and makes his own profit, offering the exporter certain guarantees in return for the exclusive rights to a given market area.

In Europe both these representation systems, plus many variants on each, are common, depending on the type of product being handled, the accepted system within the industry concerned and the stage of development of the agency company. Generally speaking, for example, if goods are to be sold from locally held stock, it is advisable for that stock to have been bought by the distributor, who is then motivated to avoid overstocking at the factory's expense.

The drawing up of an agency profile serves a number of invaluable functions: it ensures that the exporter has a clear idea of his own objectives; it reduces the chances of error in selecting the agent; it gives the potential agent more confidence in working with the exporter (European agents cannot afford to waste their time with unbusiness-like partners); and it greatly facilitates the work of any organizations called upon to help in locating potential agents.

Although to the well organized export companies, this emphasis on the agency profile might sound platitudinous, the extent to which it is necessary to stress this basic preparation is only too evident, according to executives in the Export Services Branch of the DTI, the Overseas Business Development Departments of the big banks and the export service sections of the various chambers of commerce. They all deplore the enormous amount of time and effort that is wasted through having to deal with requests for assistance where the manufacturer has made little or no efforts to define his real requirements. Consequently, when a request is received that is well documented and very specific, the chambers, the banks and the commercial officers in our embassies feel stimulated to give it that much more attention.

More than one agent per country

The publicity surrounding Britain's move into Europe has placed a great deal of emphasis on the welding of the continent into one homogeneous grouping. In fact, the one thing that can confidently be said about the Common Market is that the members have very little in common. The reduction of trade tariffs between the old and the new members will not in any way weld them into a single market. The main change is that our entry should make British goods more competitive in price within each single individual market. (At the same time, it will make their products more competitively priced inside the British market.) From a marketing point of view, therefore, there should not really be any reason for using the term EEC or Common Market in any re-organization of export marketing. After thirteen years of EEC existence, the Italians, French, Germans, Dutch and Belgians still appoint their own commission agents or distributors in each other's countries, for there has been no move towards homogeneity of language, taste, or general life-style. Nor has the EEC made the constituent populations much more fond of each other than they were in the past.

But there has been a difference in the growth of individual companies. Product marketing has very much broken out of a home-country, home-made type of atmosphere, and market leaders have sprung from completely unexpected areas in many instances as the managements have taken advantage of the offer of a much enlarged, duty-free market area. One of the surprises has been the way in which Italian manufacturers conquered so many of the markets for domestic equipment, durable consumer goods and even industrial equipment. This was partly due to the fact that they found their duty-free territory had become equal in size to that of France or Germany, both of which had previously enjoyed a much bigger, protected home market. But another factor in their success was that the Italians treated the area as a collection of very individualistic market areas, each demanding its own local subsidiary or agency coverage.

The typical dynamic exporter aiming to do a good job of maximising sales into the new EEC (now to be ten countries), will probably need separate representation in twelve to fifteen locations, not including his own home market. I would suggest, for a standard consumer product or item of industrial equipment, agents would be required separately in Oslo and Bergen for Norway, in Copenhagen for Denmark, in Dublin for the Republic of Ireland, in, say, Hamburg, Dusseldorf, Frankfurt and Munich for Germany (the options are wider in Germany – there could be three, there could even be five), in Paris and Lyons or Marseilles for France, in Amsterdam for Holland, in Brussels for Belgium and Luxembourg, and in Milan or Turin (or even both) for Italy. Even then, you could not feel that there was a guarantee of coverage of, say, the southern half of Italy, the whole of the Atlantic and Channel coast of France, the Trondheim area of Norway.

It has frequently been a sobering experience for established exporters from Britain to analyse the sources of their business from the Continent. One firm was pleased with its turnover in West Germany until it did the exercise of putting pins in the map to show the location of its customers there. None was more than 75 miles from the agents HQ in Nuremberg. Letraset Ltd is another example of a company which for the initial years was pleased with its turnover in Germany because this was so much bigger than its other export markets. However, when compared with the country's real potential, the company changed its representation there and results were multiplied.

It is possible to find agents who have branches in a number of different cities within a country. These branches must never be taken at face value, however. Very few German agency firms are strong throughout the territory, and a branch has to be discounted unless it is visited personally by the exporter and assessed separately in the way the agency HQ itself is assessed. Germany is so much a federation of separate concentrations of population and industry, that each "branch" of an agency or distributor will have the same job to do as its parent, so it should be judged with this in mind.

The separate market areas within the member countries have separate identities for a variety of reasons. In Norway it might be called "geographical"; as a result of the way the mountains run, a keen sense of separate identity exists between the Bergen and Oslo regions. In Belgium there is the linguistic and cultural difference between the Flemings and the Walloons (Flemish and French-speaking respectively), not at all keen on each others' company or language. Germany, until comparatively recent times (end of the nineteenth century) was a maze of separate principalities with only the German language in common. In France, there is a big difference in way of life due to climatic variation. Paris and its surroundings are really North European, whilst Marseilles and the Riviera and Pyrenees neighbourhoods are Mediterranean in location, tastes and attitudes.

The Marketing Director of one of Britains largest publishing companies told me that when he paid a visit personally to a book fair near Marseilles, he was overwhelmed with requests from booksellers who were simply interested in learning the names of British publishers. His own sales in Europe were being handled through two agents – one for "South Europe" and one for "North Europe" and after about ten years in the market, hardly a book had been sold to the Marseilles area. His decision to go to the area himself opened a useful market overnight. His agent had been the agent for many other British publishers, so the Marketing Director's appearance on the bookselling scene down there caused quite a stir. It was a unique opportunity for the local buyers to find out what Britain was doing.

Supervising the agents

There are many ways of organizing the supervision and control of agents in Europe. The strange thing is that few firms have actually given special thought to this. The large majority of British exporters I have interviewed over the years have tended to think that their way was the only way. There methods have not changed with time or with growth, nor have they taken stock of the situation at appointed intervals to see if there could be a better way. I have found several ways in which responsibility has been allocated to staff and agents by successful exporters.

A frequently employed arrangement is to divide Europe into segments, with an export manager or salesmen responsible for each main segment, motivating the agents within it and progressing orders received from it. For example, east Europe might be given to one expert; France, Italy, Spain and Belgium (because of the French language) to a second; Germany, Austria, Switzerland and Holland to a third, and Scandinavia to a fourth. This can work effectively, allowing individual managers to become well acquainted with a given number of agents, their best customers, the local languages and ways of conducting business. Difficulties can arise, however, if the types of outlet vary very much for different products within a given territory. For example, an Irish linen manufacturer covers Scandinavia with one salesman (working with agents in each separate Scandinavian country). This salesman finds it necessary to make entirely different sales tours for, on the one hand, domestic linen (tablecloths), and on the other hand, cloth to be made into wearing apparel (skirts and suits). Each type of selling requires exclusive concentration during its season.

Another system is to appoint exports sales managers responsible for a single product line throughout the whole area. One firm, for example, had previously divided Europe into segments but found a much better penetration possible when it used the same three men to travel to agents in every country, but each concentrating on one major line only. So instead of one man dealing in France, Italy and Spain with steel, hand tools and garage equipment, he became a specialist in selling hand tools to the whole continent, whilst his two colleagues similarly specialised in the other two lines.

A more complex but very effective method (if the right personnel is available) is to build up a bigger system of specialist distributors based on sales outlets in a given area, and have them prompted and serviced by one local agent working on commission. The advantage is that a greater number of outlets can be tapped without overstraining the resources of any single agent, and yet the lines of communication for the exporter are not too complex. He simply deals with the one local commission agent.

It is generally true that the more clearly and simply defined the objective of each single person in the export chain of marketing, the more effectively he can operate. You may end up with a situation in which the export director chases five European segment managers, who each chase five commission agents, who each chase five local distributors, who each chase their five biggest wholesale buyers. But at least, this will mean that, in a very short space of time, 625 big potential customers can be approached by individual salesmen, each very conversant with his product and on close terms with the customer, and each being motivated by someone who has only him and four other people to concentrate on. This compares favourably with the all too common system where the export director sends a memo to the European sales manager who is away in Italy. When he gets back, he reads the memo and sees that he is about to leave for Stockholm, and is then going to attend the Hanover Fair. He therefore puts a note in his diary to the effect that when he next gets an urgent telephone call from the agent in Paris (whom he was supposed to meet on this trip but he couldn't fit in), he must ask him to pull his socks up and get a bit more business from not only the industrial users of their spanners, but also from the handyman shops and, if the Paris agent happens to be in touch with the agent in Geneva (who is the Paris agent's brother-in-law, because that is how he came to be appointed) to pass the message on to him, and if there isn't a big improvement in orders for the next three months, they'll get the sack from the giant company which is about to make a bid for the British firm, because the giant firm will probably bring in consultants who will take a close look at every agent's performance!

In this nightmare, but all-too-true-to-life situation, I have not restricted the territories to those which are members of EEC, because, although I have come across many different ways of managing exports to Europe, I do not think I have ever come across anyone who was specifically in charge of exports to EEC. And to repeat the important point made at the beginning of this article, there is no reason why they should be.

LOVE THAT AGENCY

The ever-popular pastime of switching advertising agencies is wasteful of both time and money. Michael Rines sought advice on how a more stable relationship could be created and maintained between adman and client.

Choosing, briefing and living with an advertising agency is like a love affair; it is a story of courtship, proposal and marriage, and if each stage is managed effectively and tolerantly the affair should have no ending in divorce

Three men with wide experience of the advertising industry were chosen as our counsellors Nigel Seely, chairman of the agency Papert, Koening, Lois Ltd., Geoff Darby, marketing director of Beecham Foods Division, and Bill Ambrose, trade relations director of Beecham's Products Division

Nigel Seely has been on the agency side of the fence for the last seven years after spending a number of years on the client side. During twelve years with Slip Products Ltd. he was responsible for hiring and firing agencies in fourteen countries, including the US, as well as the UK.

Geoff Darby is particularly well equipped to give advice on how to get the best out of an advertising agency because he has spent about half his career on the agency side of the fence and the other half on the client side. He graduated from the Procter and Gamble school before moving to General Foods where he was involved in the launch of Maxwell House Coffee and Instant Whip. He next went to Beecham before joining McCann-Erickson, the advertising agency. From there he went to Nestlé where he set up the marketing department in their newly acquired Crosse and Blackwell subsidiary. He then went back to McCann, becoming accounts services director, before returning finally to Beecham where he handles the marketing of the group's food and health drink products.

Bill Ambrose offered an interesting contrast with Darby, having been with Beecham for 44 years. He has been connected with marketing and advertising for a large part of that time.

"When I joined the company it had only one product – the famous pill – and from this the Beecham Group has grown." Ambrose's current more specific responsibility for monitoring what goes on in the advertising world, and in particular for keeping an eye on Beecham's interests in it, was reflected in his opinion that the clients who get the best value for money are those who take a close interest in their agencies' work.

Choosing the agency

Both Darby and Ambrose agree that the first essential in choosing an agency is for the client to be clear in his own mind what he is looking for, and the two most important qualities are first-class creativity, defined by Darby quite simply as "the ability to produce ads that sell goods", and good media buying, defined as "the ability to get to the target audience as often as possible at lowest cost".

Other qualities, such as honesty and courage, are desirable too, but to Darby and Ambrose the most important are effective creativity and media buying. Seely agrees, but would rank honesty almost equally high. What he means by "honesty" is willingness to stand by ideas. Anyone can stand by facts, but ideas are incapable of proof whether they are the client's or the agency's. "If an agency doesn't agree with you, it should say so loud and clear. This often hurts because it is you who are paying, and why shouldn't you have your own way? But you are unlikely to be right all the time, so listen and try to be reasonable. If you feel you cannot stand the bonhomie of the padded agency man when he's trying to woo you, you can be sure you will find him intolerable when he is angry? So tolerate directness when you come to choose an agency, but make sure they are the type of people you don't mind disagreeing with sometimes."

The first step in choosing an agency is to draw up a short list of about six agencies. This list should be arrived at by a combination of methods. The first and most obvious step is to seek the opinions of people in the trade on both sides of the agency/client fence, the opinions of media people being particularly valuable because they are in a better position than anyone else to know how well a given agency rates in its buying of television time, or, in the case of press advertising, how well, for example, the agency uses colour. The IPA (Institute of Practitioners in Advertising) is also a valuable source of professional opinion.

Useful estimates of agencies can be made by watching advertising, either on television or in the press, and then finding out the source of any outstanding campaigns. So look for advertising ideas and try to spot how the agency has both created them and taken advantage of marketing opportunities. Differentiate between what the product has done, what the client has done, and what the agency has done. Try to delve behind the ads.

It is also worth noting which agencies have won awards; at least this is a sign of creative activity. Nearer to home, note the effect of your competitors' advertising on your own sales, because although it is not possible to use the agency concerned on your own competitive product, it is possible to sue such an agency for a different product in your range.

The growth record of an agency is a fair indication of its merits. No agency is likely to achieve significant and sustained growth unless it is doing a good job for its clients. It is a simple matter to check growth in billings of any likely agencies. And again a lot can be learned of the quality of an agency by looking at the calibre of its clients. Information on billings and on the clientele of particular agencies can be obtained from Media Expenditure and Analysis Limited.

At the presentation stage, Darby attaches most importance to the impression created on him by the people making the presentation. "I don't want to know how big they are, how many overseas offices they have and so on. I'm not interested in expensive lunches, or in the extravagant facilities they've built into their palatial offices to impress their clients, and 'do let me walk you round the agency', positively frightens me." Darby prefers to have the agency make its presentation in his offices. If the agency is good, it won't have any difficulty communicating its ideas away from the special facilities of its own premises. Ambrose likes to talk to people on an informal basis apart from the official presentation; it is a good thing to let agency specialists explain their thinking.

To Darby, the most important fact to establish at the presentation is whether or not the "chemistry" between him and the agency is likely to be right. He likens the client–agency relationship to marriage, and, as in marriage, the most frequent cause of rifts is a failure in the chemistry, the breakdown of the intangible bond of empathy between the two. "It will help to establish the right chemistry if the agency can show it is interested in us and show it has taken the trouble to learn something about our products and our company."

So Darby is judging primarily the members of the presentation team, and it is therefore vital to establish that the team facing him is the team which will handle his account and not some special performing circus drummed up with the sole purpose of selling the agency's services. Clearly there can be no objection to the presence of a senior member of the agency who may not subsequently be closely involved in the client's account, but he should confine himself strictly to introducing his team and should play little part in the presentation.

Establishing the existence of the right chemistry is not enough by itself. It is also necessary to find out the way the agency approaches its problems. The team should therefore show, in a series of four or five case histories, how they have tackled other accounts, and if these are in different fields it will demonstrate the agency's flexibility. The cases should show clearly the nature of the original problem, the research, the solution and the result.

At the presentation stage Darby does not ask the candidates to put forward proposals if the problem he is concerned with is related to a new product; the security risks of doing so are obvious. If the subject is an existing product there is, of course, no such inhibition. It is particularly valuable to hear candidates' proposals when the reason for seeking the agency is that an agency previously employed on the product in question has shown an inability to deal with its problems.

Ambrose is prepared to go further than Darby at this stage. He stresses that clients must be prepared to investigate the agencies in considerable depth. He would send someone familiar with the workings of agencies to visit them to examine their facilities, (and, equally important, to talk to the senior staff; a visit by such an expert avoids the danger of being taken-in by the convincing "blarney" the agency might put up at a presentation. Then Ambrose would put the agencies on his list to the test by asking them to carry out a full scale exercise on either a real, if possible, or an imaginary project, such as a test market. He feels it is most important to be thorough at this stage because the fate of a considerable investment is going to depend on the choice. The client must therefore be prepared to spend, and Ambrose would pay all but one of the agencies an agreed fee for carrying out his test. The only candidate who is not paid is the successful one.

Seely points out that apart from the basic agency services, there are a lot of other things that agencies do, and you may need them, e.g. marketing, research (qualitative and quantitative), public relations, economic forecasting, and even tickets for the Cup Final. Nearly all the big agencies do most of these things superbly. The smaller agencies mostly buy these services outside. If you favour a smaller agency, make sure you know what and from whom they are buying. You can, of course, buy the services yourself, but you should tell your agency what you are doing and work with them.

As an ex-client, Seely confesses to "being suspicious" of agencies that have small extra services departments, particularly in the research area. They may be excellent at prediction the potential sales of a foreign motor-car in a particular price range, but not so good when it comes to ascertaining the housewife's attitude to the acceptance of a new grocery product. A big agency with built-in additional services that are well tried is fine for you if you need them, but so is a small agency that is good at buying these services outside. "Just make sure", warns Seely, "that the agency you are considering does not put its *creative* work outside. If it does, it's a client not an agency, and that's what you are. Be cautious of middle-sized, middle-class and middle-good agencies."

Briefing the agency

A written brief is essential if the possibility of misunderstanding is to be avoided, and it should be particularly clear on the amounts and methods of remuneration. The brief should set out very clearly the client's policy in relation to the product and should provide the agency with all available relevant information. This should include, for example, sales figures, Nielson information, market research reports, and the relative importance to the client of the product in relation to the rest of his range.

The agency must know as much about the product as possible and to this end its staff should be invited to see the production lines. It must know the client's selling methods, and members of its staff should visit customers or shops with the client's salesmen, "otherwise the agency's creative people are likely to use language and pictorial effects which mean nothing to the woman in Scotland Road, Liverpool".

The agency should be encouraged to ask questions, and nothing material should be concealed from it. Darby would draw the line at passing on the formulations of his products, and would be guarded about costs and profit figures, but Ambrose would reveal more information (but not all) to persons of appropriate seniority because it could be, for example, that the agency might make a selling point out of the high cost of making the product, perhaps because it was using only the best and most expensive materials.

Seely agrees that you should tell the agency everything about your business relative to the problems that you want them to be concerned with. "If you don't come clean with them, they will find out for themselves if they are any good, and hate you for not telling them. That is your little bit of honesty. If you tell all, you can often get an involvement and dedication beyond commercial sense."

To anyone who is nervous about giving confidential information to an agency, Darby points out that in his considerable experience in dealing with new products he has never come across a case where an agency had been the source of a leak. When leaks had occurred, they had originated most often with label makers and block-makers.

Ambrose feels that it is important at the briefing stage to involve not only the creative people, but also members of other departments of the agency, such as media buyers, so that they feel involved. Darby agrees: "Its all part of the business of getting the chemistry right at the outset and it is a great advantage if the agency feels enthusiastic about the product."

Living with the agency

The frankness and freedom established during the briefing process should be continued throughout the relationship between the agency and the client. In Darby's words, "Success often depends on how well three men on one side get on with three on the other." And returning again to his analogy with marriage: "It's important that if you have a complaint against an agency you should not store it up to avoid a fuss; the longer it's put off the worse it will eventually be." Seely, on how to live with an agency, is even more emphatic: "Quite simply, love them, or if that is impossible, tell them you do. You would be surprised how agency personnel need to be appreciated."

Both Darby and Ambrose believe that there should be regular monthly contact with the agency at the client's marketing director level. It is essential that these meetings be informal, preferably over a meal, the view being taken that in the relaxed atmosphere it is easier to be frank.

At lower levels contact should be much more frequent, in appropriate cases almost daily, so that the agency can be kept completely up to date with the client's thinking. Changes in policy, for example, should be passed on immediately. Here again the relationship must be informal; large formal meetings are disastrous But though contacts should be frequent, it is important that the purpose of the contacts should be quite clearly understood to be mainly for communicating information and not for constantly amending instructions and commenting on the agency's efforts, which will rightly be seen by the agency as interference. "Give the agency a plan," says Ambrose, "and let them get on with it."

Allowing the agency to "get on with it" does not mean abdicating all control over what the agency is doing. Ambrose feels it is important, for instance, to watch them fairly closely to the extent of checking in detail on their media usage. The purpose of this watching, however, is constructive – to make it possible to hold informed discussions with the agency and, perhaps equally important, to show that you are interested.

If, in spite of the attempt to nurture a friendly atmosphere, disagreements should occur at the lower levels, it is important that they should rapidly be referred upwards and as rapidly settled.

The client should not resent criticism by the agency; it must be big enough to listen to it with an open mind. There must be complete freedom of speech. And, while Darby does not expect the agency to create his marketing policy for him, he does consult it on his marketing problems in the sense that he invites comment on his plans once they are made.

Darby has several golden rules. First, it is important that the agency should not attempt, in setting up its team, to match the structure of the client company's team working on the product. Some agencies apparently consider that they have to do this to impress the client, but it inevitably leads to the creation of a team that is much bigger than is neccessary. This is not only bad economics, but leads also to a lack of interest among the members of the agency team because none of them is able to play a big enough part to provide a satisfying role. Again, if the team is too big there are too many voices and too many layers through which ideas are filtered. This tends to result either in compromise solutions to problems or, worse, to the diversion of the campaign away from the original direction because too many amendments are made.

Darby's second rule is an insistence on the account manager being fully involved in the campaign, otherwise, once again, its direction can drift away from the original intention. Third, it is important to ensure that the creative department of the agency does not have too much autonomy. The creative ouptut must be operated under a proper control mechanism, such as a review board on which the creative director's seniority is no greater than that of the other members of the board. Fourth, the costs of any extra services to be provided by the agency must be agreed in advance.

Ambrose makes a plea that will find an echo in the hearts of many an agency in the volatile and insecure world of advertising. "If in spite of all your efforts the agency's team fails to measure up to your requirements, you can always ask them to change the team working on your account. You don't necessarily have to switch agencies." Sometimes a lot of investment has been made between client and agency. Only as a last resort should this be thrown away.

Predictably, Seely has strong views on this and makes the point that when you change an agency you take one step forward and two backwards – at least, for the first year. "Obviously, if your agency is really awful, kick yourself (or your predecessor) for hiring them in the first place, then take a close look at your own staff. Marketing managers, and particularly inexperienced brand managers, can murder good ideas from almost any agency with a ruthless precision."

Seely concluded with the adman's prayer to his god, the client: "We can, and sometimes do, move the proverbial mountain for you then one day an advertisement reproduces badly, or it offends the chairman's wife, and you forget the last seven successful campaigns and start to hate us. But even if you are completely right in your accusations, this is the time to ignore it and give us reassurance. For this is the time you may get our best work out of us. At least you will if you are that good, which you probably aren't, because you are human and fallible and as frightened as we are. But you pay us. And that's power. Don't misuse it. And though my agency together with many others, probably needs your business, think carefully before you consider moving the account. Particularly if you are a client of ours."

11

SHARE YOUR RIVAL'S SECRETS

Competitors have much to gain and little to lose by sharing marketing and other information, says Leslie Walsh of PA Management Consultants in this challenging article.

"Half the money we spend on advertising is wasted. The trouble is we don't know which half." We have all heard that one before, or something like it. Less obvious perhaps, is its market research corollary: "Half the money we spend on market research is wasted, and the trouble is we *do* know which half – it's the half we spend on finding out information which our competitors could give us for nothing, if only they chose to do so." If you are already exchanging market information with your competitors, either informally or on a regular and continuing basis, this article is not for you. If you are not, and especially if the mere idea seems preposterous – as it does, unfortunately, to so many marketing executives – then read on. You may save your company some money.

In fact, one of the more important and more obvious steps in almost any market research project should be an approach to one's competitors, to obtain from them such information as they are able or willing to give. Why do so many marketing executives fail to do just that? The first reason, one suspects, is quite simply that they are afraid of a rebuff. And let's be under no illusion: very often they will get one, a very firm one, but then, no harm has been done, and the number of market researchers seriously injured in the course of competitor approaches is, up to the present time, zero. Why not have a go?

But let us assume that you are not rebuffed. You may well gain information of immense value, information that no other avenue of research could provide. This is particularly true in the new product field, especially where initial capital investment is necessarily high. Other methods of research may reveal a growth market simply waiting to be exploited; what they cannot always reveal is the intention of other companies to enter the same field, with resultant overcrowding and cut-throat competition right from the start. The position is much the same with technological innovation. Companies are often quite prepared to reveal at least something of their research if they realise you are likely to have a competing product to put you on the market – if only to discourage you. This kind of information is often unobtainable by any other honestly conducted method of research.

Honestly conducted? Is there not something underhand, in any case, in an approach to competitors? The answer, very firmly, is "no". The ethical position is perhaps not quite as clear as it might be, although it has been thrashed out in various codes of conduct issued by relevant professional bodies. Whilst these codes on the one hand emphasise the need to ensure that informants are in no way adversely affected by the enquiry, they do permit the use of cover names by research agencies, provided they are registered with the Department of Trade and Industry, thus enabling informants to locate such company names if they wish. This use of cover names does seem to allow scope for less scrupulous practices, especially as the average informant in unlikely even to be aware of the proviso, let alone take advantage of it. Perhaps there is scope for a more categoric pronouncement by the professional bodies. In the meantime, common sense suggests a simple rule: that the approach should be open, with no subterfuges, no cover stories and no false identities.

If you wish to use an agency or consultancy to preserve your anonymity, you may do so, but you must allow the agency to make it clear at competitor interviews that the research has been commissioned by a competitor or potential competitor of the informant company. Unfortunately – and this is perhaps why so many companies view the competitor interview with distaste – not all companies maintain clear ethical standards. Agencies get to know the approach: "What's all this rigmarole about sampling frames? I'm a simple man myself, all I want is for you to get hold of my competitors' order books and analyse them for me. And I'm prepared to pay good money for that." This sort of request is accompanied as a rule by a jocular guffaw. The agency will join in the laugh and return to the problem of the sampling frame; the competitor interview has not even the remotest connection with industrial espionage.

Nor, it should be emphasized, has it anything to do with illegal collusion. Some years ago the Restrictive Trade Practices Act would be mentioned – quite unjustifiably – in this context. Now the bogey is the European Community's rules of competition. The Commission of the European Community, however, has made it quite clear that "an exchange of opinion or experience", or "joint market research" are quite outside the scope of Article 85 of the Rome Treaty (the principal article dealing with restrictive practices).

In fact, it is in the international field where the competitor interview is most likely to pay off. International market research expenditure always seems to be too tightly stretched over too many markets – never more so than at the present time, with imminent UK entry into the EEC. And, to the extent that it is possible to generalize, it seems that the foreign company is much more inclined to co-operate – companies in the US, W. Germany and Italy can usually be relied on for a particularly favourable response.

But what, you may well ask, is the value of the information obtained from competitors? Is there not a danger that we may be led up the garden path? Well, we must not be naive: we must face the fact that we are living in a hard, competitive world and that the danger of false information does exist. We should be foolish not to cross-check every item of information we possibly can – after all, the essence of industrial market research is cross-checking with several different sources, such as raw material suppliers, original equipment manufacturers, component suppliers, distributors and end-users. Competitors are only one such source, though often an extremely valuable one, and deliberate dishonesty is usually easy to detect – and, in a properly conducted research project, almost automatically detected.

In all fairness, it should be pointed out that cases of dishonesty or deception are extremely rare. The "reply churlish" or the "countercheck quarrelsome" are more usual than the "lie direct". Few informants have the nerve – or, indeed, the skill – to carry through a blatant lie for the the full-length personal interview. (Avoid mere telephone interviews if you can.) Fewer still have the gall of the managing director who declared his lack of faith in his trade association's market size returns. He was quite certain that the other companies fiddled their figures – at least, he fiddled his, and he reckoned he was more honest than most of them. On the other hand, while you may normally expect nothing but the truth, you cannot hope for the whole truth. No competitor can be expected to reveal his hand entirely.

But will not competitors, in return for helping you, expect some information in return? Indeed they will, and this you must be prepared to provide. There cannot be a one-way flow; there must be an exchange.

Let us assume that you are prepared to provide this information, that you are convinced of the value of the competitor interview. How should you set about it, assuming no previous contact? A few simple guide-lines may be derived largely from what has been said so far:

1. Make it clear right at the start, that you are a competitor.

2. Make it clear that you are offering an exchange of information, not asking for something for nothing.

3. Make it a personal interview, not just a telephone interview, if you possibly can.

4. At the interview, act as though the approach is for you a perfectly normal one in market research – which it should be, even if it is not. Do not, on the one hand, seem to be asking a favour; on the other, don't appear furtive or self-conscious.

5. More important than in other types of interview, leave your sensitive questions until the end of the interview. At some stage, if you are taking full advantage of the interview, you will probably come up against a refusal – there is no point in meeting it at too early a stage.

6. Give information as you receive it, but watch out for the wily informant whose aim is to pump you dry without giving anything in return.

7. *Accept information as subject to cross-check, especially in areas of obvious self-interest. It is posssible to begin your cross-checks tactfully with the informant himself during the interview.*

8. *If the interview is a success, consider regular and formal contact in the future.*

Sometimes, even a rebuff can provide you with information of value. Take, for instance, the case of the specialist food manufacturer: "You've got a nerve, haven't you? Ringing up for an interview to find out the size of the market. You must know that's practically tantamount to asking what our turnover is." (This in the days before disclosure of turnover in company accounts.) "We have over 96 per cent of the UK market, you know. You researchers are all the same. Like newspaper reporters. Why only the other day, a reporter rang up while the Board were all at a meeting, asked a sales clerk for our turnover, and then published it! What newspaper would do a thing like that, you say? Why, the *Daily Blurb*, last Wednesday." It cannot surely be unethical to take advantage of a man like that.

But perhaps the competitor interview is still not for you? Well, it's an ill wind that blows nobody any good. You have at least the consolation that you are God's gift to the market research business.

12

MODIFY PRODUCTS
FOR PROFIT

Most writing on product planning concentrates on new product development, product pricing and product elimination. Here, John Winkler sets out seven ways to modify existing products for bigger profits. He says that constant tiny changes can keep nudging up sales, reduce costs and increase margins. But such a process needs a well thought out marketing approach. The article has been adapted from the author's book, Winkler on marketing planning, *published by Cassell/Associated Business Programmes.*

A company's product mix sets the upper limit for its potential profitability. The quality of the company's marketing programme determines how far this limit is reached. Therefore there are two factors to adjust constantly in order to optimise profits. One is the product range, and the other is the marketing programme to support the product range. The term "product planning" embraces both of these factors at the same time and is at the core of company profitability.

Products within the range are constantly being modified; more often than not by managers outside the marketing function. For example, different classes of raw materials are purchased from time to time, yielding different quality levels. Alterations in production systems, or in quality control, provide different product results.

Changes in distribution systems may affect product quality, in terms of freshness, or breakage. Countless pressures are exerted on all products every day, and strictly these should result in only marginal changes. All these changes should be within the levels of tolerance agreed by the marketing function as being acceptable in relation to competitive standards.

Most marketing texts concentrate on the heavy end of the product planning process. They are concerned with new product development, product pricing or product elimination. Few texts concentrate on those changes that go on all the time within the product mix; those often tiny product modifications which can constantly nudge up the profits in terms of increased sales, reduced costs, or raised prices.

Seven possible alternatives present themselves when modifying products. The use of each technique is dependent upon the circumstances of the products in relation to the buyer, matched with the product objective of sales and profits.

1. *Quality improvement*. Most managements seek to improve product quality constantly, in the belief that this will strengthen their competitive position. However, the deliberate and sustained effort to build in extra "quality" as perceived by the engineer, through the use of, say, higher grade materials, may not achieve the desired effect of increasing "quality" as perceived by the buyer. There are four levels of quality improvement in descending order of effect on the market.

(*a*) Improvement that is perceived as such by a significant number of buyers, in both the appearance of the product and in its performance.

(*b*) Improvement that is not visually observable by a significant number of buyers, but is one they detect in improved product performance once they try it.

(*c*) Improvement in quality that is aimed at a specialised end-use and only of significance to a proportion of the buyers.

(*d*) Improvement to the product that not only cannot be perceived visually, but cannot be detected in the product function. The existence of such an improvement must be taken on trust by the buyer. Many improved proprietary medicines come into this category.

In seeking constantly to improve product performance a company may modify its product quality in each of the four ways at the same time. This explains why some modified products are easier to "force" into the market than others.

For example, the meat products company Henry Telfer Ltd. produces many improved products for the catering trade each year. Most recently it has introduced a range of simulated steak products using an American process. These have been immensely successful because they represent a vast improvement upon the normal hamburgers and they look and taste like steaks while being considerably cheaper. All of this is obvious to the buyer in the product presentation.

A year ago Telfer re-launched an improved formula for its cooked meats range. These needed more sales and marketing pressure because in order to demonstrate the improved eating qualities of the products, buyers had to taste them first.

The company also sells saveloys in fair quantity, a sausage-type product that has no national market potential, because its appeal is to a tiny market sector in one area of the country.

Finally, the most difficult product improvement is the alteration of a basic recipe in, say, a pie product. If the meat is cut into chunks instead of being minced, it takes a long time for the market to realize that a change has been made because the difference in taste and appearance is marginal.

2. Feature improvement. This aims at increasing the number of real or imagined product benefits. The first cameras were bulky, heavy things. With an improvement in lenses and shutters, a series of alternative speeds was made available, and miniature versions were developed. This led on to built-in range finders, then built-in exposures meters and flash connections. Such feature improvements are designed to increase the range and scale of the products use. They can be adapted to appeal to special segments of the market.

3. Style improvements. This aims at improving the aesthetic appeal of the product, rather than its functional performance. In certain classes of goods it may be the critical factor governing the buyer's choice, and excellent styling may even outweigh some functional disadvantages. For example, very fine glassware needs to be handled with exreme care (one disadvantage), and it is expensive (another disadvantage), but it appeals to our sense of fashion or taste.

Colour, shape and texture are the three most common variables when developing style improvements. In repeat purchase markets, style improvements may be limited to packaging or pack design. Nearly all buyers, including those in industrial companies, respond to good, clear presentation. Even when tendering for contracts, companies using glossy presentations have been known to edge out bids from companies that present themselves poorly.

Style improvements need not be exclusive of other product improvements. And they can often be introduced with little additional expense at the development stage, provided thought and care is devoted to the problem.

4. *Value analysis.* This seeks to change the formulation of the product in such a way as to improve the performance, or at the least to hold it constant, while reducing the cost. The intrinsic worth of each component part of a product and the function it has to perform is questioned and analysed. Typically, most products are made of some materials that are scarce or costly. The replacement of these materials by a lower grade or cheaper alternative may horrify the engineers or production executives, but if it does not affect the performance of the product in relation to the customer's expectations, then the company has little cause to worry about the change.

The value analysis technique has been developed to great lengths in the past few years, encouraged by pressures on company profit margins. A little care needs to be exercised over its continuous application since, though one small modification may not be felt, the cumulative effect of a series of modifications may be detectable within the product performance.

5. *Product degradation.* One of the effects of price wars, rapid inflation and declining markets is to reduce the product quality. In order to stay in business a company will trim quality from the product to cheapen it, or to maintain its profitability. Bit by bit it goes until the product performance is affected and is noticed by the buyers. Industrywide, all the products under profit pressure will be produced down to the lowest level of quality the customer, the

standards authorities or the law will allow – and some will go lower than that, through widening their specification tolerances. This is what everyone fears when quality levels are reduced.

Product degradation may, however, be a desirable manoeuvre and may not have harmful effects on the market. For example, most basic quality standards are set by the production function – whatever marketing management may say. The production men are the only ones who are expert enough to nominate the alternative levels of quality in a new product from which we, in marketing can choose. They build in quality safety-levels. And so products are often made to quality standards not desired by the market but are to shore-up production risks. They are, in fact over-engineered. Therefore in most products there are wasteful components and materials which are of peripheral interest to the buyer. Packaging often comes into this category. These items can be altered and the products "degraded" safely.

6. *Service improvement*. Service improvement is often employed by smaller companies competing with large organizations. Service may mean providing technical advice, more frequent delivery, faster supply, breaking bulk, consultancy help, and after sales support. The problem with service improvement is that if it works, then competitors tend to copy. It may also be expensive to apply. Service improvements usually appeal only to a sector of the market; and they work best where the chosen service is the outstanding weakness in competitive organizations. When service standards are already high in a market, it pays to look eleswhere for product improvement.

7. *Promotional benefits*. Some companies, particularly those operating in price competitive markets (usually those with undifferentiated products) seek to add value to their products through the addition of promotional benefits. Give-aways, competitions, collector premiums, invitations to the company's holiday home on the Mediterranean – all serve primarily as short term inducements to buy. But some product fields have become so inundated with promotion activities that they have become a regular part of the product offerings. Incentive schemes have a tendency to make buyers switch brands more, and in undifferentiated product fields a

significant number of them will often switch primarily for the special offer.

An example of product planning

Broads Builders' Merchants Ltd. is a private company centred in London. It sells building and decorating materials to the building trade and householder. The product lines vary from paints and water taps to manhole covers. Broads specializes in the provision of heavy-duty ware, e.g. bricks and drainage materials for trade users, such as building contractors.

Initially the company acted as a merchant but gradual re-organization resulted in the formation of a holding company, Broad and Co. with two subsidiary companies, one of which was a manufacturing company, the other being in the merchanting business. It is the latter that is dealt with in this case study.

The problems

Originally the company had developed in the traditional fashion of builders' merchants, having a poor consumer image and show-rooms of interest only to builders and architects. Gradually the company was restructed to place emphasis on the various depots. In this way the depots increased their individual buying power and responsibility for meeting market needs. By rationalizing stocks over all the depots and by tying the whole organization to a stock-list the advantages in buying and selling gradually gained momentum. During this time the first moves were made by the company towards the establishment of a self-service department and more professional displays in the showrooms.

The solution

Whilst the new policies were beginning to work, the various departments lacked cohesion and more impetus was required in sales. The return on investment was still too low. It was decided, therefore, to appoint a marketing manager and to form a marketing division. The Division was able to build results on the work that had already been initiated in three main areas:

(a) Stocks were geared to minimum stock turn levels.

(b) The Marketing Division became responsible for overall buying policy – thus the assessment and satisfaction of demand became a continuous process.

(c) The sales force became totally involved with the product range carried by the individual depots.

The traditional market, the builder, lacked immediate growth potential. Expansions was achieved by:

(a) Taking the self-service department that had been started in 1967 and widening its stock range to appeal to the "do-it-yourself" customer. Colourful decoration and up-to-date merchandizing assisted this aim.

(b) Introducing associated products, such as fitted bedroom and kitchen furniture, tiles, timber and own-brand products, thereby widening the product range.

(c) Transforming the showroom into a "Bathroom and Kitchen Design Centre" with improved displays. A consultancy service was also added to advise customers on kitchen layout, with a service to design their kitchens, if they wished.

Advertising was stepped up. This aimed at the Londoner especially, and the Underground was therefore used. Direct mail shots became a standard form of publicity to customer and potential customer.

Results

In the 18 months following the implementation of the new policy the following results have been observed:

(a) For the latter 10 months of 1970 the budgeted figure was beaten by 3 per cent, and for 1971 the present trends show that the results will be 19 per cent up on 1970. The average rate of growth since reorganization is 12 per cent per annum.

(b) The company is more marketing orientated.

(c) Personnel are working as a team towards common objectives.

(d) The company is able to recognize and profit from changing demand patterns.

KILLING COMPETITION

Most companies accept the need to know their markets, but many of them fail to realize the importance of knowing and acting against their competitors. Michael Clay and Michael Rines explain what can be done.

Although many companies have marketing policies and even occasionally written marketing policy statements, there can be few marketing managers who have detached themselves completely from the pressures of day to day operations to develop a strategy covering relationships with competitors. Marketing actions in this field tend to develop as a result of short-term trends, such as a series of orders lost on price or service, rather than as part of a planned offensive campaign. The efforts of sales managers, planners and salesmen are usually concentrated on establishing good quality products, on providing good service and on selling at a fair price. The danger is that these admittedly necessary functions may be carried out in a competitive void as if competitors do not exist, as if the only occasion when the competition needs to be recognised is when the company finds its performance is slipping against its own plan.

There are a number of reasons why one needs to know a good deal about the enemy:

1. It is difficult to judge your own performance if you are not able to relate it to the opposition. For example, you might feel satisfied with a growth in turnover of four per cent per year if you did not know that the leaders in your trade were achieving eight per cent. Again, you might be satisfied with a margin of 10 per cent, but not if your rivals were achieving 15 per cent.

Disappointing though such discoveries might be, they are probably symptomatic of something worse. They almost certainly mean that there is something seriously wrong with management or plant and that the company's position is likely to get even worse, rather to than stay static in relation to the competition. And what happens if the market contracts and a bout of price cutting starts? It means the company will be making a loss while the opposition may still be making a profit. In fact, if the enemy knows enough about you he can force you out of business almost any time he likes, simply by cutting prices.

2. Price is, of course, only one of the tools of competition, and it is equally important to know what standards are being achieved in the way of product design, performance and service generally. It goes without saying that if the competition develops significant advantages over your product, you are in trouble. The important thing is to make sure that you know about it *before* the product is launched. Again, if delivery times are shorter than yours, or are more reliably maintained, you need to know. And the same is true if improved distribution arrangements, such as the setting up of local stock points, are being made. In fact, there are few activities of an opponent which do not affect you in some way. If you can get advance warning of new developments it means you are better armed to combat them or even to pre-empt them.

3. So far we have been looking at the situation from a defensive point of view, but it is, of course, equally important to have a knowledge of your competitor's weaknesses so that you can take advantage of them.

4. It is important too to keep an up-to-date picture of a rival company in case another rival makes a bid for him. Such a take-over could result in the creation of a new company of a size that would render your situation perilous. It is, therefore, necessary to be able to react swiftly to any such bid and to have sufficient information on hand to make a prompt counter-bid possible. Indeed, the possession of adequate information might either prompt you to take the initiative in making bids, or might even enable you better to fight off an attempt to take over your own company.

The range of information required

Many companies would benefit from a complete rethinking of policy on competition. In the first stage of the exercise, one should completely ignore any legal restrictions, informal price agreements, current trading relationships with competitors, problems of monopoly, or any other difficulties in the way of the new policy. This ensures that your thinking is uninhibited and that you fully realize the range of weapons available. At a later stage, you can decide what you are prepared to sacrifice in observing the conventions.

The principal indicator of success in battle is the share of the market actually achieved and its relative profitability. The detailed activities described below should be geared to a marketing plan which specifies the share of the market expected and the expected position in the league of competitor profitabilities.

It is desirable to set down the information about competitors that the company would like to possess if there were no restrictions of cost, legality, confidentiality or of any other kind. This information will include, for each competitor:

1. Product information

A complete list of all the competitive products in his range with comprehensive details of their design, properties, analysis and performance. Engineering drawings, samples, models, operating and maintenance instructions, installation instructions and a full range of sales and technical literature should be available for each. In particular, a careful analysis of competitive products should be made.

2. Customer information

A complete list of all important customers and potential customers should be compiled, showing details of amounts purchased. A dossier on each customer should show his credit worthiness, size of individual orders, special peculiarities and the names of purchasing decision makers. This information would be of most value for those customers who are not served by the company and on whom little information will probably be available.

3. Marketing information

Information should be collected on the type of selling effort made by each competitor, the number of representatives, the sales regions, the policy on remuneration of salesmen, full details of the advertising carried out and the promotional aids available.

A comprehensive picture is needed of the standard of customer service offered. How much after sales wervice is given? What is the policy on breakages and rejects, how much technical effort does each competitor make available? What is the delivery period and how many products are met from stock? What does each competitor know about the activities of its competitors? What special strengths and weaknesses exist in the marketing efforts of each competitor?

4. Cost and profit information

Is anything known about competitors' costs, contributions and profits? What selling prices are given to different customers? Are prices standardised, i.e. quoted from a price list or calculated on a basis of what the market or customer will bear? What is the estimated break-even point? How easily could they withstand a price war? What is the financial strength of each competitor and his rate of profit on sales and on capital? In what ways is the company financially vulnerable, e.g. to devaluation, to a take-over, to a price cut?

5. Production information

What is each competitor's productive capacity? How many products does he make which do not compete with ours? What proportion are these of the total effort? What processing methods are used and are these better than ours?

6. Personnel information

Details should be obtained of key executives in competitor organizations, particularly those in marketing, but also any other specially valuable or indispensable managers. How vulnerable is the competitor to executive poaching (head hunting)?

7. Legal information

Records should be kept of important patents filed, and of licensing and royalty arrangements made.

In addition to static information about a competitor at one point in time, the company will require a full dynamic picture, i.e. each competitor's plans, objectives and progress. Such information can be collected under the same headings as those listed above:

(*a*) *Products: new product development and product rationalization plans*

(*b*) *Customers: plans to increase or decrease the range of customers served*

(*c*) *Marketing: future advertising campaigns*

(*d*) *Cost and profit: investment plans*

(*e*) *Production: process developments; research and development progress and plans*

(*f*) *Legal: patents or applications being considered.*

How to obtain the information

The items described and listed above are not exhaustive but cover most aspects of a competitor's operations in which the company may be interested. The next two major questions for the company, and for the marketing function in particular, are what methods of information acquisition is it prepared to countenance and on how many of the above aspects does it want to be briefed. The second question is the easier to answer. To mount a serious and thorough competitor offensive, marketing needs at least some information on all the headings.

The first question involves questions of legality, of ethics, of the nebulous transition zone between industrial intelligence and industrial espionage. In deciding what means are permissible the company will need to tread carefully. A useful starting-point for the compilation of such a list has been prepared by Worth Wade, a Philadelphia management consultant. The first seven items in the Wade list are unquestionably ethical and legal. Thereafter the list is approximately in a descending order of acceptability, and each company must make its own decision about the methods it is prepared to use. As a general guide it is suggested that any method that is legally available to a member of the general public is ethically acceptable.

(*a*) *Published material, and public documents such as court records.*

(*b*) *Disclosures made by competitors' employees, and obtained without subterfuge.*

(*c*) *Market surveys and consultants' reports.*

(*d*) *Financial reports, and brokers' research surveys.*

(*e*) *Trade fairs, exhibits and competitors' brochures.*

(*f*) *Analysis of competitors' products.*

(*g*) *Reports of your salesmen and purchasing agents.*

(*h*) *Legitimate employment interviews with people who have worked for competitors.*

(*i*) *Camouflage questioning and "drawing out" of competitors' employees at trade and technical meetings.*

(*j*) *Direct observation under secret conditions.*

(*k*) *False job interviews with competitors' employees (i.e. where there is no real intent to hire).*

(*l*) *False negotiations with competitor for licence.*

(*m*) *Hiring a professional investigator to obtain a specific piece of information.*

(*n*) *Hiring an employee away from the competitor, to get specific know-how.*

(*o*) *Trespassing on competitors' property.*

(*p*) *Bribing competitors' suppliers or employees.*

(*q*) *"Planting" an agent on competitors' payroll.*

(*r*) *Eavesdropping on competitors (e.g. via wire-tapping).*

(*s*) *Theft or photocopying of drawings, samples, documents and similar property.*

(*t*) *Blackmail and extortion.*

What information should you collect and how should you go about collecting it? It will be essential to appoint someone to be responsible for collecting the information on a systematic basis, even though in smaller companies it may have to be done on a part-time basis. It does not really matter much who the person is so long as he is sufficiently bright and experienced to be able to see when he has got hold of something significant. It is probably preferable for him to be a marketing man because much of the information will be of a marketing nature.

The fact that he will be required to keep financial information as well as information on, for example, production capacities, does not debar him because he can either learn to interpret it or can take it to the specialists for interpretation. Once appointed, it must be made clear to everyone in the company that everything learned about a competitor must be passed to him, even though it may seem insignificant – so very often two separate insignificant facts become significant when added together. The actual organ-ization and management of an intelligence function is well documented and consequently need not detain us here. References are offered for follow-up reading on this subject at the end of this article.

The information can come from almost anyone in the organiza-tion, ranging from a member of the purchasing department who is urged by a supplier to buy a piece of new equipment because a competitor has just done so, to a report from a technician that the competitor is advertising for a number of technical staff. Even a lorry driver might hear in a transport café that the competitor is opening a new depot. The systematic collection of such informa-tion does not take up a lot of time and can obviously be of immense value in providing early warnings. Such information is picked up very much on an *ad hoc* basis, however, and there is much more that can be learned by careful and planned analysis.

Perhaps the most valuable source of information is your compe-titor's annual report, particularly if it is a sizeable public company that uses the report as a public relations tool. The annual report will also indicate related companies, either parent, subsidiary or associated, and will list the shareholdings of the directors. Within the file at Companies House, but not in the report, can be found a full list of shareholders, and what you find there can be of obvious significance. For example, you may find that the majority of the shares are owned by one family, or most of them might be held by one man who you know to be very old. If this is so, there is a strong possibility that he might be tempted to sell, or that when he dies his successors might be tempted. On the other hand, if the share-owning family still has members involved in running the company and drawing a salary from it, a takeover is likely to be that much more difficult. Useful information and interpretation can also often be had from reports in publications like *The Financial Times* and *The Investor's Chronicle*.

This leads on to the point that in these days there are many excellent business and management publications which devote considerable space to company profiles and industry surveys. It is possible to pick up a lot of information about some companies at the cost of a phone call to the editorial offices of some of the magazines. You will find that most of them keep indexes that enable them quickly to refer you to the issues in which relevant articles appear. Another invaluable source of information is the trade association of the company in which you are interested. Such an organization is usually quite ready to supply information as part of its public relations effort and if you are yourself a member it will probably supply a useful range of statistics about the industry and its members.

Another source of information that it is easy to overlook is the competitor's local newspaper. You may find information in this that you cannot find anywhere else. For example, if your competitor has a strike it is likely that a report will appear there, but not in the national press. And if your competitor does have a strike this is a splendid opportunity for you to cash in (a discussion on the morality of this is outside the scope of this article). Again, the local paper may report items such as an application for planning permission for a new factory building, and later on may report its official opening by some civic dignity. The same paper will also carry job ads which can give a clue to planned expansion. So place an order for that local paper and see that someone skims through it every day.

A further important way of finding out about your competitor's activities is to go and have a look at his premises, from the outside. There is nothing whatever unethical about this if you accept the criterion that it is perfectly legitimate to take advantage of any information that is available to the public at large. This may sound an absurd thing to do, yet simply by standing outside a factory the following information can be gathered:

(*a*) *Locations of buildings which can, when related to a large-scale Ordnance Survey map, provide a very accurate guide to the dimensions of the site and of individual buildings. It will also show whether there is room for expansion on the site, and in some cases you will see evidence that new building is starting.*

(*b*) *The age and condition of the buildings can be estimated, and the use to which they are put can often be detected from their nature, e.g. the presence or absence of chimneys or distillation columns of an appropriate kind.*

(*c*) *With the above information on the size of the site and the quality of the buildings, it is possible to obtain from a local valuer an estimate of the sale value of the premises.*

(*d*) *You may see products coming out of the factory you did not know your competitor made, and you may be able to see the extent of his stocks if they are of the kind that are stored outside.*

(*e*) *The transport going in and out of his premises may tell you who his suppliers are, who his customers are and whether or not he runs his own transport. The amount of material being shipped out of the factory may also give some clues to production or sales volumes.*

(*f*) *It may be possible to learn something about working methods, e.g. it will be easy to see whether or not the factory is run on a three-shift basis.*

Lastly, having got all this information, it is necessary to make full use of it. This requires the involvement of top management and there is an obvious case for having "competitor activities" as a standing item on the agenda of every executive and board meeting.

By continuous monitoring of the activities of a competitor, it will be possible to build up, not just a factual documentary, but also a knowledge of the way he is likely to act in a given situation. It is possible, so to speak, to build up a knowledge of his personality and this can be of immense value in predicting his reactions to, for example, the launch of a new product by you or a price cut. Why not try it? You will be amazed how much you can find out at very little cost, and why not give the job to someone you are anxious to develop? Learning about the competition and analysing their businesses is an admirable training project.

The offensive strategy

The next and the most vital step in the entire procedure is the development of an offensive strategy against competitors. An offensive strategy is a plan that aims to interfere with a competitors' operations, and reduce his performance in any directions. It includes hundreds of possible actions from imitating his products to bombing his factory. Again, every company has a problem in deciding which offensive tactics it finds unacceptable. Also, the methods which a small company would tend to use in harrying a large and powerful market leader (product imitation, head hunting) would tend to differ from the reverse situation in which a large producer wishes to eliminate a small one (e.g. large loyalty rebates, price cuts in the small man's market area). Here again, therefore, a decision has to be made. In studying the following sample of offensive strategies one should remember that these two types of choice are necessary before the list can be used and also that it is only a sample or perhaps a foundation upon which each company must build its own comprehensive list.

A competitor can be attacked via any of the resources used (materials, manpower, mind-power, machines, money) or generated (products, customer loyalty and goodwill). Alternatively one can plan an attack via his marketing operations, financial operations, production operations, or service operations (e.g. R. & D., personnel, legal).

Attack on products

(a) A very useful method is to imitate the competitor's product so closely that the average consumer cannot detect the difference. Advantage is taken of the competitor's research, development and market knowledge but the difficulty lies in the speed with which one can get into production. Sometimes it may even be advisable to market a cheap imitation which will fail or otherwise disappoint a purchaser to bring the competitor's product into disrepute. Product imitation has been one of the basic forms of competitive attack used by Japanese industry for many years.

(*b*) Closely evaluate the features of the competitor's products and pass this information to representatives in a suitable form for them to attack competitor's products when they meet customers. Some firms have very detailed booklets on competitor's machines in which all their weaknesses and strengths, but particularly the former, are elaborated.

(*c*) Try to arrange for special import duties to be levied on competitive products on the grounds of dumping or unfair competition or for other reason. If competitor's products contain harmful or dangerous features it may be possible to arrange for the supplier to be prosecuted.

(*d*) Introduce a better product.

Attack on raw materials

(*a*) Buy all the available material by contract.

(*b*) Persuade raw material suppliers to increase prices to competitors, or not to supply them.

(*c*) Purchase the companies that supply the raw materials in order to control the supply.

Attack competitor's marketing operations

(*a*) Show customers as clearly as possible how weak the competitor is on product availability, lead time, after-sales service, etc. Show customer that the competitor supplies others at lower prices.

(*b*) Persuade overseas agents not to handle competitors' goods or to handle them passively.

(*c*) Find out details of competitor's forthcoming advertising campaigns and anticipate them by advertisements which will make the subsequent appearance of the competitor's advertisement look foolish or appear to be plagiarisms.

(*d*) Arrange for subsidiary or related company to purchase from the competitor and inundate him with complaints.

Attack competitor's financial operations

(*a*) Deliberately involve competitor in costly law suits which weaken his financial strength. This was one of the prime methods used by Paterson in developing the National Cash Register Company in the early years of this century.

(*b*) Purchase product or materials or services and hold back on payment.

(*c*) Arrange that the competitor's share prices become depressed so that the public become reluctant to invest.

(*d*) Ask other companies who supply the competitor how promptly their bills are paid. This may cause them to press for payment.

Charles Grutzner, "How to lock out the Mafia," *Harvard Business Review*, March/April 1970.

P. I. Slee-Smith, *Industrial intelligence and espionage*, Business Books.

Peter Hamilton, *Espionage and subversion in an industrial society*, Hutchinson.

14

HOW NOT TO GO IT ALONE

The advantages and disadvantages, and the do's and don't's of joint ventures are explained by Richard Bickers, author of Marketing in Europe, *who is now running a marketing consultancy.*

Joint ventures are held in suspicion by most businessmen, but they are, in certain circumstances, an excellent way of entering a new market or expanding within a given market sector.

Suspicion arises firstly because it seems obvious that if two (or more) companies have equal interests in a joint operation, neither can exercise the control essential for efficient management. Secondly, wariness is created by the knowledge that joint ventures are always difficult on account of the high degree of tact, diplomacy, give-and-take, and sensitivity to other parties' feelings demanded of the partners. Joint ventures by more than two partners are, for this reason above all, infrequent and not to be recommended. Two companies coming together for a common operation are faced with enough problems, but at least enjoy better prospects of harmony than if there are more parties involved.

If joint ventures are fraught with potential conflict between partners of the same nationality, it is manifest that the dangers of disagreement are multiplied when the arrangement is being negotiated and then conducted by companies from different countries. Cultural differences tend to become exaggerated. There are conflicts between varying standards of ethics and business practice, there are national characteristics such as pride and obstinacy to deal with, and there are even differences in sense of humour that can ruin a relationship. And this daunting list takes for granted the basic essential of lucid communication; unless perfect linguistic understanding has been established, the union has no hope of being put together, let alone managed, effectively. This is particularly important where the initial agreement is concerned. It must be taut and unambiguous, and good lawyers on both sides are as important as negotiators, accountants and technical experts.

Despite the problems, what makes joint ventures worth while in the right circumstances is the profitability that can be achieved by two companies sharing complementary attributes. Joint ventures should therefore be considered alongside the more usual systems of distribution: through agents or distributors, wholly-owned subsidiaries or branches, licensees, or franchises. And they need not be limited to the marketing activity; manufacturing, servicing or assembly joint ventures are practicable, even independently of a company's marketing strategy.

Where a joint venture is advantageous

The circumstances in which a joint venture might be advantageous arise:

1. When a small company wishing to enter a foreign market lacks the capital, manpower or marketing skill to do so on its own, but in exchange can offer technical ability.

2. In a country where total foreign ownership of a company is not permitted, and this method is therefore the only alternative to selling through agents or distributors.

3. When it will qualify for preferential treatment given only to companies owned, wholly or partly, by nationals. Such preference may take the form of a generous allocation of foreign exchange, government contracts, the speedy installation of utilities or construction of buildings, development grants and subsidies.

4. Where the political environment is such that it is desirable to have a native partner in order to enjoy some degree of protection against the vicissitudes of government policy. These may occur not only with a change of administration, but also during the tenure of office by one party over a long period.

5. If a company is perceived to be losing its grip on a market through under-capitalization, poor quality products or any other weakness. If its goodwill still exists, another company might be able to build on the former's established reputation by providing the very qualities needed to rescue it.

6. When a manufacturer has spare production capacity and seeks rapid expansion into a foreign market. A joint venture with a company already marketing there would save the time needed to set up a new marketing organization.

7. To surmount tariff barriers or to take advantage of membership of such communities as EEC, EFTA, LAFTA.

8. When a company operating overseas wishes to involve local management in the fullest manner. A joint venture could provide a greater degree of independence and participation than a branch or subsidiary.

9. To provide the most attractive incentive to a partner to exert his best efforts, e.g. when it will encourage him to match the first party's technical or financial contribution with his own production or marketing skill; and, in an international joint venture, call on his national pride.

10. As the only way to make good an otherwise unfillable gap in the overseas strategy, i.e. opening the door to a foreign market by local partnership in assembly, warehousing, or after-sales service.

11. When manufacturing overseas is the cheapest way in which to supply other markets.

12. When, for maximum profitability, an individual market or a group of markets must be operated in isolation.

To the small company there can be particular appeal in a joint venture with a big company as partner, particularly in an overseas market. This is because it is not necessarily the partner with the most to offer that obtains some of the greatest benefits. By being integrated with a global plan, the smaller partner inevitably shares in the financial profitability of, and acquires knowhow from, the marketing operations of its bigger partner.

Objections to joint ventures

The two major objections to joint ventures are:

1. The acknowledged difficulty of mating two separate companies, whether of the same nationality or not in a commercial marriage bed. A disproportionate amount of time is likely to be spent on resolving disputes and the management of a jointly owned company is perhaps forced to adopt compromises and play each principal off against the other with resultant confusion of purpose.

2. They lack flexibility. Becoming a partner in a joint venture entails important long-range implications. It is necessary to take into account a company's global marketing and investment strategies. Long-term profitability in the frequently changing conditions of international markets calls for flexibility. Joint ventures are inherently inflexible because they create difficulties in the integration or rationalization of multinational production, give rise to special problems of taxation, and may reveal that the corporate objectives of the partners are incompatible.

An example of the last-mentioned weakness in joint venturing would arise, for instance if a British company with a wholly-owned subsidiary in Holland and partnership in a joint venture in Italy, manufacturing the same product in both countries, were to receive an order for it from America. If the product could be supplied at the same price and the same profit margin from either source, the British company would be in a predicament. It may have excellent reasons for giving the business to its Dutch subsidiary, but its Italian joint venture partner is unlikely to be sympathetic.

Another dilemma would face a British manufacturer exporting products to distributors throughout the Middle East who then goes in for a joint venture in Iran to produce and market the same range under a different label. Such a company would be in competition with itself in the most uneconomic way. There may, of course, be strong reasons for such action, but great care is needed in such a delicate situation.

Another danger that confronts a partner in a joint venture is that he may be creating future competition for himself by introducing sophisticated management, manufacturing or marketing techniques into areas where they are unknown. He may find he has trained employees who will later set up their own companies and use these very techniques against him.

The conflict of interests between a joint venture in one country and the international operations of one of the partners in the venture becomes most serious when the latter sets out to regionalize production. This was the experience of an American company which had set up both majority- and minority-owned joint ventures in several European countries. None of these manufactured the complete product range, but each made a large segment of it. With the establishment of the EEC the American company found that in five of the member countries its joint ventures were competing with each other. Clearly, the solution was to rationalize production. The other shareholders in each of the countries concerned, however, refused to accept this: they were not concerned with what was best for the whole international operation of their American partner, but only with what was advantageous to themselves. In consequence, a European holding company had to be formed, and shares in this given in exchange for shares in the various European joint venture companies. Had the American company set up a wholly-owned operation in each market, in the first place, it would certainly have been able to allot production of different finished goods or components wherever it wished; but, in defence of the joint venture concept, it must be said that it would not have been able to enter so many markets so soon.

How to maintain control

Wherever possible, a company which initiates a joint venture, whether at home or abroad, should set out with the intention of securing and maintaining control. This can be done in many ways, of which some are as follows:

1. By issuing both voting and non-voting shares, so that even though both partners may hold 50 per cent and enjoy half the profits, it has the majority voting in power.

2. By providing, in the agreement, that it will have a majority on the board.

3. By securing for itself the power to appoint management.

4. By each partner holding 49 per cent of the equity and the remaining two per cent being held by a third party who will vote on its side.

5. By agreement that it shall have the casting vote in a tie.

6. By having a management contract with the joint venture company.

7. By controlling a marketing company to which the total production of the joint company must be sold.

8. If the joint venture is being set up only to meet legal local participation requirements in a foreign market:

(a) The local partner can be a bank or insurance company which will take no part in the management.

(b) The necessary local shareholding can be put on the market and thus dispersed publicly in such a way that there can be no effective counter-voting block.

Despite the case against joint ventures, some 65 per cent of the 100 biggest British companies are partners in operations of this type. Cynics may say that this is the most powerful advocacy against them, but most businessmen would probably agree that, if the giants see enough advantages in joint ventures to compensate for their admitted drawbacks, smaller companies may benefit similarly.

Some examples

It is very unlikely that Shell-Mex and BP, United Glass (Owens-Illinois and Distillers), British Aircraft Corporation (GEC and Vickers) or Mitsubishi Heavy Industries and Chrysler would have taken this route unless it provided them with optimum profitability.

It was by means of a joint venture that Shell broke into the Italian petrochemical industry: supplying the funds which Montecatini, strong in research and management, needed and could not obtain in the difficult Italian capital market. Also,

General Electric took advantage of Machines Bull's lack of working capital to supply this need and, with Bull's first-class marketing set-up, formed a viable joint venture.

Mitsubishi Heavy Industries, having been concerned entirely with engineering, while the Mitsubishi group's own trading company handled all its marketing, first entered joint ventures with Caterpillar Tractor and then Borg-Warner to market earth-moving equipment and industrial refrigeration equipment, respectively. In the US Mitsubishi Heavy Industries thus benefited from its partners' expertise in marketing and after-sales service. Now, the motor vehicles division of Mitsubishi having been formed into a separate company, a joint venture has been set up with Chrysler in which the latter began with 15 per cent participation and an option to increase this to 35 per cent. Not only is the company currently exporting some 4,000 units a month to America, but sales in Japan have also increased greatly.

A good example of a company opting for a joint venture in an overseas market in which it was forbidden to have a majority shareholding, yet effectively controlling the operation despite this, was provided by Corning Glass in India. In return for cash investment it was allowed 39 per cent and for its technical contribution a further 10 per cent. Of the remaining 51 per cent, half was taken up by the Indian partner and half put on the stock market. Thus, despite its minority position, Corning Glass was in the seat of power because 25.5 per cent of the possible vote against it was widely spread.

Perhaps the most friendly way of handling a joint venture is to set up two companies, one to manufacture and one to market, with the equity divided 51/49 per cent and 49/51 per cent respectively, between the partners. In the cleaning industry, which, in addition to contract cleaning firms, embraces the manufacture of machines, chemical products, and a constantly growing range of mops, buckets, wringers and equipment trolleys of increasing sophistication for the cleaning and maintenance of industrial, institutional and hospital premises, an interesting recent joint venture has been established on these lines.

The biggest contract cleaning organization in the world is

Danish and employs 30,000 cleaning staff in Scandinavia alone. This company, Det Danske Renøgring Service, also manufactures a range of cleaning equipment under the name of Darenas and owns another Danish company manufacturing industrial chemical cleaning products. Det Danske Renøgring Service is now engaged on a series of joint ventures with Electrolux to cover both contract cleaning and the manufacturing and supply of machines and other cleaning products. Where a contract cleaning business is established, the Danish partner holds 51 per cent and Electrolux 49 per cent of the equity. Where a marketing operation is set up, the shareholding ratio is reversed. By this means, a world-wide comprehensive cleaning and marketing operation has been made possible.

The construction of a joint venture agreement offers wide scope for the exercise of negotiating skill, and when it is between partners from different countries it can be one of the most worthwhile contributions marketing executives can make to international relations. The essential qualities, in addition to experience and subtlety in this type of bargaining, are the ability to remain unruffled, to be resilient and to be tolerant without being weak. Perhaps, above all, toughness is needed, for the long-term implications of a joint venture mean that a negotiator is committing his company to a future in which its position must be strong from the outset.

There are many control techniques open to those who enter joint ventures, in addition to those already listed. These may be established through patent and trademark rights; rotating chairmanship of the joint company (as in the Italian venture by Finsider and US Steel); agreements for continuing contributions of know-how, production, or service; or an option agreement. The last has two uses: firstly, to enable the partner who enjoys it to increase his equity by an agreed amount in the future; secondly as a threat that he *will* do so if the other partner does not comply with his wishes should a confrontation arise. Monsanto is a good example of a company that has obtained, and exercised, equity options on more than one occasion in its European joint ventures.

As a final recommendation, an international joint venture

agreement should provide that disputes between the partners will be decided in a third country, to ensure impartiality: Switzerland, or the International Court at The Hague are good choices.

Conclusion

And as a final stricture for those involved in negotiating and conducting a joint venture: toughness of purpose and unfailing courtesy towards the other fellow are the indispensable virtues. It is rather like a ball game, really, and as the British invented sport, we should be the world's best joint-venturers.

15

THINK BEFORE
YOU CUT THE PRICE

Industrial manufacturers very often accept that their products are almost identical with those of their competitors. And when this is so it is often thought the only way to compete is the self-defeating price cut. The present article, which is from an Industrial Market Research Ltd. monograph, gives the reasons why it pays to think before you cut your price. Jeremy Fowler led the IMR team.

Non-differentiated industrial products are products made to a standard or fixed specification, bought only in response to basic and essential needs, and used in markets where purchasing decisions are governed in the main by rational factors. Examples are computer reels and cases, electro-mechanical relays, electric wire fittings, cables, drills, ball valves, plastic tubing, hand tools, plywood and laboratory glassware. All these are, in a marketing sense, similar to salt or detergents. The characteristic of such products is that it is very difficult to find any feature of the product itself which gives a competitive advantage. So much so, that many manufacturers have come to believe that price cutting is the only competitive weapon available. All too often it is used with results that bring no long-term benefits to the company concerned and lasting damage to the profits of whole industries. The consumer goods marketing answer has been to build into products of this type perceptual rather than fundamental physical differences, for example by virtue of unusual design, by packaging, by endowing the product with psychological rather than physical attributes or, most important of all, by branding.

And, however far fitted hose may be from hose fittings and cheese-spread from chipboard, there appear to be good reasons for examining if there are some techniques used in the raucous consumer goods markets which might be applied, with profit, to the more restrained industrial markets.

Pipes and hose fittings share, along with a large number of industrial goods, the problems of non-differentiated products. Almost all are indistinguishable from other products of the same type, either because of competitive pressure to manufacture to a given level of performance or appearance, or because of the adoption of national or international standards. Either way, the situation appears to leave little room for product adjustment. This article shows that there are in fact many means which can be used by a manufacturing company to distinguish its goods and services from all others.

Characteristics of non-differentiated products

The approaches for marketing non-differentiated products are numerous but none can be selected or implemented unless the basic characteristics of these types of products and their markets are understood in some detail. They are products:

1. whose users prefer and seek lower prices rather than improved products;

2. whose use confers no significant financial or technical benefits as against the use of any other of the genus;

3. whose purchase offers no corporate or personal prestige.

No benefits accrue from the introduction of product "plusses" which in fact lead to a downward pressure on prices. For example, the majority of chipboard buyers would not pay one penny more for twice the quality since they use the minimum specification compatible with their needs. If a producer offered a better quality at the same price as the current product, the customer would seek a lower price on the unmodified product.

Similarly, while a particular hand power tool may be demonstrably superior in some respects to competitive products, it is extremely difficult to distinguish a standard bit from any other bit.

Finally a computer, a new factory or a new communication system may endow the firm with a more favourable image of promotional advantage, but a concrete pipe or a standard valve fulfils a utilitarian function and nothing else.

Buyers of non-differentiated products

How then can a manufacturer of an industrial product produced to a standard specification, in a market that buys only when it must, obtain a competitive lead? The answer since price collusion became illegal, has most frequently been "price cutting" or price cutting in its very worst commercial and social form – bribery. Such policies are as injurious as they are unnecessary, and are often destructive for the purchaser as well as for the seller. Price cutting is a philosophy of desperation based on an ignorance of marketing and of market forces.

It is a constant jibe that every industrial buyer seeks to purchase at half the price, twice the quality and delivery from stock. All three propositions have been shown on serious investigation not to be true. The book *How British Industry Buys* and its American and Canadian equivalents clearly demonstrate that:

1. A significant number of buyers would not switch from their best supplier for a price drop often as high as 10 per cent, because buyers not only buy products: they buy security.

2. Value analysis could not have achieved the huge (and quantified) success it has if products were not frequently over-designed (i.e. to high a quality for the purpose for which they are required).

3. Study after study has shown that buyers most frequently want assured *delivery, not* quick *delivery.*

These factors should be recognized since they open up the way for developing techniques to establish market leadership by removing some aspects of buyer–seller folk-lore which inhibit creativity in industrial marketing.

The study of purchasing attitudes can be broken down into three major areas: deciding *who* buys, *how* they buy and *why* they buy.

With non-differentiated products the buyer tends to be the

purchasing officer, since the purchasing takes on the characteristics of repeat purchases or straight re-buys. Information requirements are low, and consideration of alternatives is also low. Because there is no innovation content in the purchase, the purchasing decision is a fairly simple one involving lower levels of management only. But if the seller can introduce an aspect of innovation into his offer, which will in any way change the *status quo* in the buying firm, he can force the consideration of alternatives and perhaps move the decision into the responsibility area of others who may favour the company. "Innovation" in this context can be related to commercial terms, product applications, reciprocal trading and other non-product aspects of the transaction. Similarly, if there is early knowledge of the initiation of the purchasing process it is possible to influence the specification and the search for suppliers. Finally, given that buyers (particularly in non-differentiated product markets) do not buy the products but the cluster of satisfactions with which they are surrounded, a knowledge of buyer motivations makes it feasible to present the offering in a manner which most closely accords to what they seek to purchase.

The knowledge of the buying processes dovetails with the need for executive selling discussed later, since the sooner in the buying process the selling company is involved, the greater becomes the need to work with senior management on the buying side, and thus to engage in executive selling. The buying processes are complex and sometimes difficult to understand, but knowledge of them places the market oriented company in a far better posture for completing a sale than their more pedestrian rivals.

Search for uniqueness and the innovative content

Any attempt at product differentiation, to be successful, requires consideration of two important factors. The first of these is the concept of uniqueness and the innovative content of any offer, and the second, the product and its market fit.

An essential primary requirement is to develop some aspect of uniqueness, if not in the product itself (which by definition cannot be differentiated), then in its surrounding services, commercial characteristics or any other activity which impinges on the successful operations of the customer firm or its well-being.

It is the factor of uniqueness which opens up the prospect of exceptional profits even for non-differentiated products, *not* the latest tool, which any competitor can buy and operate, *not* large sums of money available, because finance can be acquired at a price, *not* cheap labour, *not* good procurement practices; all these, alone or together, might ensure what could seem to pass for a respectable performance, but introduce the element of uniqueness and that resource or skill can be transmuted to gold by its creative exploitation. A unique operating skill makes a work a day machine exceptional, a unique way of manipulating funds, of purchasing or of utilizing labour, separates profit earners in the top quartile from all others.

The development of the use of uniqueness, of course, places a firm at risk which means that it can make either high profits or high losses, since in a risk situation both results are possible. What is certain is that while losses can always occur, profits are only likely to be exceptional if a degree of uniqueness can be achieved and the firm is willing to embrace risk in its exploitation.

It is obvious that the opportunity for achieving uniqueness in most aspects of a company's operations is limited. However, there remains one area where opportunities for uniqueness are myriad, where pay-off can be quick and where rewards of leadership can be high. This area is marketing, for in non-differentiated industrial products it is marketing that has been least practised, least understood and least appreciated, because it has been thought that it is inapplicable in a situation where everyone is selling the same product.

Competition, as has already been pointed out, tends to centre around price which is the least flexible, the most destructive and non-creative use of an important marketing weapon. By the use of the full range of marketing tools which are available to the producer of industrial goods it becomes possible to invest the firm and the product with a "plus" which cannot easily be followed by competitors. The greater the number of unique elements or the degree of innovation which can be introduced in an offer, the greater the value sensitivity of buyers becomes. This situation often eliminates and always reduces price pressure.

Product and market fit

Every firm must consider precisely how the existing standard product meets the market's real requirements. Although the market may have accepted the standard, it does not necessarily mean that it prefers it to other alternatives. It has been commented with some truth that product development and marketing orientation ceases when a BSI or an ISO specification is accepted. These standards, however, often represent no more than minimal guidance and protection to the buyer and reflect a consensus of committee opinion designed to satisfy the least exacting member of the committee.

The position is perhaps understandable since, although BSI committees are supposed to be composed of representatives of firms making the product, of user companies and sometimes of trade organisations, user companies frequently take so little interest that in practice manufacturing companies dominate the committees. One result of this is that some users will purchase to the appropriate British Standard with regard to test methods, but fix their own acceptance limits. For example, while electric light bulbs are made to a standard of 1,000 hours it is recognized that there is no difficulty, with an insignificant increase in costs, in making 2,000 hour bulbs and there are now claims for unlimited life.

Opportunities for differentiating standard products without inducing price changes abound if the manufacturers do not assume the standard is *preferred* as opposed to *accepted*. Marketing research will provide a profile of user needs, both tangible and intangible, which at least enables a supplier to direct his R & D, his manufacturing processes and his marketing towards meeting something more than an acceptable minimum. Marketing research often reveals that products are over-designed for their intended use. Indeed, the success of the technique of value analysis often proves this. By reducing the extent of over-design it is often possible to introduce more important benefits without an increase in price.

Application engineering and second use

A tendency exists in non-differentiated product markets to assume that the applications for the product are limited to its major and conventional use. In fact, although concrete pipes, for example, are used largely for drainage and water movement, a limited study showed a further 23 uses, some of which have been successfully exploited. A spring balancer for spot welding guns was found to command a substantial market within abattoirs and tanneries.

Plastic-lined paper sacks, biscuit tins and other forms of packaging frequently have a second life for purposes other than those for which they were intended. The second life features can be made part of the product, or at the very least provide a useful advertising medium.

Product arrogance, prejudice and history all tend to make companies manufacturing non-differentiated products assume that all known uses have been exploited. There is ample evidence to show that this view is often incorrect. The fecundity of the human mind is truly surprising, and it takes only one person to devise a new use or modification for an old product to open up whole new market segments.

The study of new uses for a product should be one of the major and continuing activities for all firms in non-differentiated product markets, since the rewards of open-minded searching are considerable. Thus it is in marketing, and in what might be termed the first of the marketing tools – industrial marketing research – that the major opportunities lie for setting the conditions of market leadership in an undifferentiated product situation.

Different markets and differentiated marketing

The process of developing competitive "plusses" must begin with a study of the basic purchasing propositions, which with non-differentiated products will be largely the same. However, the first approach to establishing a difference is to examine whether the purchasing proposition can be subjected to what may be a unique, creative interpretation of that proposition. It is a basic rule of all marketing that the marketer should identify his "plusses" and that part of his market to which those "plusses" are most meaningful. While all products of a particular genre may contain the same characteristics, the emphasis on the existence of any one, or grouping of them, to one target segment of the market can readily create an association in the mind of the purchaser between product and supplier in a way which distingiushes them from all other suppliers.

A firm of removers and packers specializing in works of art and antiques successfully marketed its services to manufacturers of sensitive instruments and fragile equipment. The heavy cost of damage in all these product groups and the need for special equipment had a similarity, if only perceptual, of requirements and thus presented the opportunity to transfer the "plus" from one market segment to another. If the product or its non-product factors have varying appeals to each segment of the market, it follows that the way of presenting these appeals will differ if only because the exposure, buying methods and needs of the segments also differ. A product which may be most economically sold through builders' merchants to builders could well require direct selling to engineering concerns. Similarly, offices buying lithograph machines may respond to diversionary pricing tactics;[1] a printing company is highly unlikely to do so.

The role of marketing is to see the purchasing appeal(s) of a product-orientated viewpoint, but from that of the would-be purchasers, and to interpret them in terms of benefits to the purchaser. Differences between essentially similar products sharing the same basic purchasing proposition can be achieved by the reinterpretation of the proposition. In essence this is a matter of thinking creatively about the product and its use and meaning

[1] Diversionary pricing tactics – image of low prices developed on a limited range of well publicized products which "rubs off" on the total operation.

to the purchaser. The process of market segmentation by market or product preferences or perceptual characteristics is well known, but the concomitant of differentiated marketing tools to promote differentiated advantages is not widely practised.

Development of a cluster of non-product advantages

It is now almost a decade since Theodore Levitt propounded the view that in highly competitive situations the process of getting and keeping customers requires that the generic product must be augmented in order to sell well, that is, the product must be defined broadly in terms of the whole cluster of satellite attributes which produce distinct customer satisfactions. To do this an effort must be made to find out what the customer wants and values, and equally as important, to identify satisfactions which he may not as yet be able to express.

Non-product advantages which can be built into a non-differentiated product are numerous but they will rarely stem from sheer inspiration. The source of ideas for non-product features must come from the market, and thus information on users' attitudes and needs, both total and limited, must be probed. For example:

1. Can the method of delivery be made compatible with the customer's handling facilities (or lack of them) or commercial needs, perhaps by the supply or loan of handling equipment?

2. Will a self-imposed penalty clause for unreliable delivery move purchasers from present suppliers?

3. Would the provision of management aids improve the customer's operation? There is a well-documented precedent for this: International Mineral & Chemical Corporation offered its customers, who were manufacturers of fertilizers, help in selling its fertilizers.

4. Can end-user knowledge be improved to encourage sales of the intermediate supplier? A Dutch glass fibre manufacturer developed an educational campaign among architects, builders and contractors to extend the use and knowledge of glass fibre building products as an aid to their fabricator and moulder customers.

The list of possible non-product advantages is a lengthy one and can be developed both by a study of the buyers and by internal examination of a company's own strengths, so that they can be exploited fully in the market place. Some other non-product factors justifying more detailed consideration are guarantee improvement, capture of a major distributive channel, high quality selling, and image development.

Guarantee improvement

With industrial products, guarantees and warranties are not usually a feature of the sales approach. There is an in-built and usually quite erroneous view that the buyer is at least as know-ledgeable as the seller, and can therefore make his own judgements without any need for guarantees, and, in any case, the latter has a reserve defence under the Sale of Goods Acts and the Trade Descriptions Act.

A realistic appraisal of the product, and even a slight insight into buyer motivations, indicates that guarantees can be used as a potent method of differentiating products. Security, notably job security, is a fundamental desire of everyone, buyers no less than sellers, and anything that enhances security commands attention and support. Guarantees offer additional security to the purchaser, provided they are presented in the correct way. A guarantee which is as long and as unequivocal as possible is a public affirmation of faith in the product by the supplier and, for the quality product, manoeuvres any competitive battle on to a terrain where it can be fought to the best advantage of the supplying company.

However, guarantees alone are of little use. Witness the cynicism of the average motorist towards the guarantees of the motor industry, compared with the wide support and approval Marks & Spencer obtains by its policy of changing products virtually without question and without any formal guarantee. For most manufacturers of non-differentiated products these are the extremes. A guarantee as a competitive weapon must first be seen to exist, second to have no "small print", and third to be honoured in its implementation.

A cursory examination of most guarantees and an analysis of guarantee claims will show that they can be safely extended for

Is the product we manufacture non-differentiated?

- ☐ do product "plusses", when introduced, lead to price cutting?
- ☐ are there any significant cost benefits to the user offered by our product compared with others?
- ☐ are there personnel prestige factors involved in the purchase of our product?

What alternative tactics exist other than price-cuting?

- ☐ how much would we need to lower our prices in order to obtain significant new business?
- ☐ is our product over-designed?
- ☐ do the buyers of our product want quick or assured delivery?

What do we not know about our products and their markets?

- ☐ is our product unique in any way?
- ☐ does our product specification fit the market needs?
- ☐ do different products require different marketing factors?
- ☐ do we fully understand the buying process?

How can we use this information to develop a cluster of non-product advantages?

- ☐ can our guarantees be improved?
- ☐ are there alternative methods of distribution?
- ☐ could high quality selling show significant benefits?
- ☐ is there an opportunity for applications engineering?
- ☐ how can our image be developed?

considerably longer periods and many of the restraints can be removed. Price wars are destructive; guarantee wars are creative since they encourage the improvement of both product and after-sales service.

Capture of a major distributive channel

The right relationship with a distributor may represent the difference between success and failure in many markets, such as in building materials, motor accessories, engineers' consumables, office equipment and supplies, electrical fittings, many timber products and photographic goods. The capture of a major distributive channel not only ensures outlets for the supplier's products but can also block competition or restrain it. The National Coal Board's widespread network of builders' merchants, for example, ensures outlets for its building products such as bricks.

"Capture" however does not necessarily imply acquisition, although this is the most obvious route. Other methods of distribution channels control exist. Solus trading as practised in the oil industry, whereby special discounts are given in return for stocking only the product of the supplier, makes it uneconomic to trade with competitors of the main supplier.

Franchising is another technique which can lead to the domination of the distribution channels. These contractual arrangements between supplier and outlet ensure that the franchisor's goods are stocked, merchandised or serviced in strict accordance with the manufacturer's requirements. The most obvious and perhaps public example of this is operated by J. Lyons. The Wimpy franchise pre-empts the largest proportion of raw material purchases by the outlets and removes them from competitive attack. Although the outlets in this case are retail units, the buying situation as between Wimpy Bar operators and J. Lyons is an industrial one.

It can of course be argued that for many firms the acquisition or tying in of a distributive network to absorb a product is somewhat akin to having a suit made specially to match a button that has been found. While this might be valid where a wide range of products all commanding different distribution systems or direct sales is concerned, it is certainly not so for a large number of companies whose major output goes through homogeneous distributors.

In terms of non-differentiated products the availability of the product through a particular distributor or distributive chain may be the factor that distinguishes it from its competitors. Indeed in some cases the reputation and image of the distributor will "rub off" on to the product, giving it what might be termed a "patina" which cannot be copied by other similar products.

High quality selling

Manufacturers often reduce the quality of the sales force in markets where products are similar, largely because prices tend to move towards cost and the salesman is seen as an order taker whose job is to arrive at the buyer's office when an order is about to be placed. It is argued that because there is no difference between products, the buyer purchases at the most convenient moment, which might happen to be when the salesman calls. This view is as primitive as it is incorrect. Non-differentiated products require high quality selling, and indeed often executive selling.

When all other things are equal, as indeed they tend to be in non-differentiated product markets, the buyer purchases from the salesman he prefers – and that after all is what personal selling is largely about. The salesman he prefers, apart from any personal charisma, will be the one who offers the greatest security, is enthusiastic and businesslike, and on whom he knows he can rely for support, Conveying this quality is the major sales task and not one to be left to order takers, and unsure or reluctant salesmen. Thus with non-differentiated products, the supplying company will always do well to consider how it can up-grade its sales force beyond that of its competitors, rather than reduce costs by using less than the best.

Image development and prestige spin-off

Image factors are extremely important in non-differentiated

product markets, because buyers' perceptions of products and suppliers are major influencing factors in many buying decisions. Tied in with a knowledge of buying practices and attitudes, the most meaningful image development can be undertaken. Moreover, a strong positive image identification strengths the "instant recall" or association factor whereby a company thinking of purchasing a product immediately links it with a particular supplying firm. There is little doubt that to most buyers there is an immediate association between Lansing Bagnall and fork lift trucks, Letraset and "instant lettering", JCB and excavators, Accles & Pollock and tubes. Other makes may be bought, but the firm first recalled clearly has some major advantages.

Because perceptions play such an important role in differentiating products, there is considerable advantage to be gained from a linking with a well-known differentiated product or a prestigious customer. Thus, although lithography machines can be differentiated by the technically experienced, to the uniformed users they are largely similar. Gestetner's contract to supply the Vatican and the private audience granted by the Pope to members of the organization certainly lifted it above the common run of printing equipment suppliers. The product may be non-differentiated, but the customer is, and thus the product is not one of a group of largely similar products but one which was supplied to the Vatican.

The ability of a product to provide satisfactions resulting from the user's perception of the social and personal meaning of the product in consumer terms, and the commercial and corporate meanings in business terms, thus offers a further opportunity for differentiation. While products may be similar, images are not.

Conclusion

By definition, the problem of non-differentiated products is to distinguish them from all others of the same class or *genre*. Price cutting will not do this.

What this article argues is that even though the product itself cannot be distinguished, it is possible to distinguish other factors that will influence its sale. A knowledge of one's products and markets will rapidly reveal what non-product aspects can be promoted and offered as a real "plus" to the buyer. Knowledge of the buying process and of buyers, applications engineering, non-product advantages such as guarantees, distribution channel control, high quality selling and image factors, represent but a small number of avenues for investigation. The firm manufacturing non-differentiated products need not adopt price cutting as the only expedient, nor is it at the mercy of the market. Indeed, as one marketing man has written: "The firm that is at the mercy of its customers deserves sympathy and nothing else."

16

REVIVING A DYING PRODUCT

New product launches are out of favour in a tough business climate; instead, more business from already existing products is the order of the day. But firms often go about it piecemeal. Here, Bryan Andrews of Bowman/Harris/Andrews, the product and market development consultants, explains some of the techniques involved in a scientific approach to product revitalization, and gives some examples.

In the hard economics of today's business climate, managements are anxiously looking for new ways of achieving increased profits without heavy investment. This has led to a more cautious approach to new products than has been seen in this country for some time and to a hard scrutiny of costs in advertising budgets and market reaserch. The emphasis in product terms has swung over to consideration of how to achieve additional business from existing products. No doubt the pendulum will swing back to new products as more investment money becomes available and as companies find a new confidence in risk ventures.

Of course, there are products from which no amount of ingenuity will squeeze more profits. They may rightly be judged to have reached their maximum potential and to have kept pace with changing market requirements. But there are many other products which can be creatively re-exploited or revitalized. Obvious candidates for revitalization are those already showing signs of slipping off the maturity line of their product life cycle or which are already in decline. Realistically, it is necessary to accept that some products have already slipped too far and are best written-off or milked.

Most companies are engaged in revitalization all the time. New packaging, a new advertising campaign or a new merchandizing activity all have the aim of increasing sales and revitalizing the brand. However, for really effective revitalization the piecemeal approach is less than satisfactory.

Techniques of revitalization

If the redevelopment of a product is a serious proposition, a revitalization plan demands many of the characteristics involved in new product development. Objectivity is important, and it can be incredibly difficult to take an unblinkered view of a familiar problem. A systematic approach can maximize the chances of taking the right revitalization decisions.

Rapid changes in shopping habits, consumer tastes, new product innovation, design and packaging, technological development, all have a cumulative effect on established products. Existing products are often sent into premature decline, not because the basic product is totally unacceptable, but because it has not kept pace with change in, say, its image, formulation or design. The problem is to unravel the significant effects of change from the marginal ones, and find the policy which will recycle the product in line with the most relevant changed market forces.

In order to identify the most promising revitalization strategy, one must detach oneself from the everyday reality and marketing mythology of the brand. Even philosophers find this state of mind difficult to achieve, so pity the poor line manager! The best way of achieving a detached frame of mind is to use techniques which help objectivity, the most suitable techniques being a spin-off from new product work. However, in revitalisation one at least has the advantage of dealing with a product with a history.

With an objective and systematic diagnosis it is possible to get closer to the roots of a product's problem than with less structured methods. One technique which we have developed seeks to isolate those factors which characterise the "most" and the "least" successful products in a market. In identifying these characteristics one has a key to understanding the mechanics of the market and this key can be strategically exploited in a revitalization plan. In real life one does not find neat bundles of characteristics common to success or failure – if it were that easy the ingredients of success would be so easily spotted that an analytical approach would be superfluous. In real life a systematic analysis brings to the surface certain common trends of success/failure which are not easily recognizable by a less formalized approach.

To carry out a typical analysis, it is necessary to draw up a list of important characteristics ranging across product features, psychological benefits and market appeal. These characteristics, of which examples are given below, are plotted on a 5-point grid with extreme descriptions of each factor in the left- and right-hand columns:

+2 +1	0 —1 —2
Very convenient	Very inconvinient
Strong flavour	Bland flavour
Modern packaging	Old-fashioned packaging

Products in direct or indirect competition are slotted into the appropriate grids. This kind of analysis should ideally be based on research data, but where this is not available to cover all characteristics there is no harm done in basing the positionings on judgement, *providing the assumptions are spelt out*. They can then be verified later by research where the positions are subsequently shown to be critical to a correct conclusion.

Another important step in the diagnostic stage is to examine the product in relation to its market and in relation to changing market demand forces in a less structured way than the analytical approach allows. Here the aim must be to assess the extent to which external forces have impacted on the product. Areas that usually need to be considered are:

(a) Changing economic trends
(b) Sociological trends
(c) Changing consumer tastes
(d) Changes in distribution systems
(e) New product introductions
(f) Changing competitive strategies
(g) Changing advertising themes/expenditures

(*h*) New packaging developments
(*i*) Technological developments
(*j*) Price changes
(*k*) Design/styling changes

This product/market analysis will help bring into the open the areas in which a product has failed to keep pace with change or areas for beneficial changes in the marketing mix.

At the end of a diagnostic study it is possible to isolate alternative action options for a revitalization programme. There is rarely *one* single action that needs to be taken for successful revitalization. Usually there are three or more desirable actions, some of which will make a bigger contribution than the others, but each of which add up to a total strategy. The diagnosis stage aims to identify which mix of options has the highest probability of achieving the required goals. Action options that are normally considered are:

(*a*) Product modification
(*b*) Range extension
(*c*) New distribution
(*d*) New sizes
(*e*) Pricing policy
(*f*) New packaging
(*g*) New user groups
(*h*) New image
(*i*) New advertising concept
(*j*) Joint venture development
(*k*) Export opportunities

As in new product development, action options are meaningful only in relation to a particular company's abilities. It is therefore useful to relate the options to the strengths and weaknesses of the company to isolate the actions which are most practical to implement and most attractive as market opportunities.

Revitalization: often the better first step

Revitalization approached in this way not only produces ideas for further exploitation of the company's most valuable asset – its existing products – but also leads to a much better definition of the role of new products in securing new profits. Revitalization is often a better first step in building short-term profits, but, longer term, new products are still usually required. When this is so, the risk in new product development can be further reduced by having a cushion of safer development in familiar markets and by providing the necessary lead time needed to get significant new products into the market place.

The co-ordination of revitalization and new product development can be a worthwhile step in maximizing the contribution of both. Both require an objective appraisal removed from the pressures of the operational management of the business, and both demand systematic analysis and creative imagination to make them a success. Above all, both serve the common goal of securing the long term growth of a company.

A case study in revitalization

A manufacturer had been puzzled by the decline in one of its products which had once been the largest seller in its list. The product had stubbornly resisted all attempts to halt a decline trend in spite of increased advertising expenditure, changing copy themes and advertising agencies. It was recognized that the pack was not exactly up to date, but the product was extremely convenient to use and fitted into the trend to growth in convenience products.

The diagnosis began by establishing a broader definition of competition than had been used before. The whole spectrum of products which could be consumed as a replacement for Brand X, in the home and outside, was analysed and the relative satisfactions they could offer were ranked against the satisfactions of Brand X. The competition was defined into several different groups of products ranging from those in direct competition, those with considerable overlap and those with fringe overlap.

Using this more broadly defined competitive spectrum a product analysis was carried out. The findings were particularly surprising to the company which had not previously noticed that some of the less obvious characteristics of the brand leaders, and of two recently successful new products, were different from its brand.

This was particularly so on dimensions of taste, flavour and pack size/price ratio. It also seemed likely that the old-fashioned pack was now working against the brand to an even greater extent than the management had thought.

A review of social trends showed that the family size profile of loyal users of Brand X hand changed. This same group were also spending more per ounce on products *other* than Brand X than they used to in the past. In other words the price differential between Brand X and its main competition had widened further than a straightforward analysis of price lists would indicate.

Having noted these warning signs, a trade research was carried out. This showed that whereas in the past the retailer was willing to take a large stock, now that the volume had slipped it was becoming a marginal product. Its shape was awkward for stacking and prevented optimum use of shelf space and this aggravated the situation by dampening the retailer's enthusiasm for taking more than minimum stock cover.

There was also little doubt that the long-term trends were against the product – its strengths were amongst older C2DE's in the north. Any new strategy would have to take account of this long-term erosion potential.

At this stage some of the options for revitalization had begun to crystalize:

Flavour:	strengthening the taste
Pack design:	modernizing design
	changing shape
Price:	change pack/size ratio
	increase price
New users:	target for a new user group with similar consumption habits to loyal users
Other users:	exploit potential of other uses

A screen was devised to assess the market appeal of the different options and their suitability for the company implement. Some of the factors considered in the screen were:

(*a*) Long-term prospects
(*b*) Long-term security

(c) Short-term gains
(d) Investment needs
(e) Danger of losing existing users
(f) Fit with company facilities and skills
(g) Fit with existing company image

Three actions came out as particularly attractive and these were in the areas of taste, packaging, and pricing policy. A revitalization programme was devised to implement the different actions independently so that their effect could be measured. First indications from controlled tests are very hopeful showing a lift in interest in the product for the first time. For longer term development, the study also produced ideas for line extensions capitalizing on "other use" potential of the product. It also threw up other new products capitalizing on the brand name and moving it to a more modern franchise for the future.

Faced with a declining profit situation and yet finding it difficult to introduce substantial new products quickly enough to offset this decline, the revitalization programme creates the opportunity to recapture lost sales at a relatively low investment risk.

The management has appreciated the benefits of this more systematic approach to reviving products. To quote the marketing director: "We spend a lot of time improving distribution penetration, stock cover and consumer offtake, and have invested in market research and testing advertising. Without doing these things consistently over the years there is no doubt that the brand would have been beyond saving long ago. But this, to us, rather unusual way of looking at familiar problems has opened up ideas for redevelopment which I don't think we can be blamed for missing by the more conventional way of reviewing tactics for the brand."

Revitalization in the market place

Without being intimately acquainted with a product's objectives, any comment on its achievements can be only superficial. Nevertheless, the examples shown in the following list spring to mind as worthy of some comment. The views offered are, of course, entirely subjective.

Smiths Crisps: With the entry of Golden Wonder was forced into an energetic revitalization programme to update product and image. Possibly would have modernized brand eventually anyway, but an interesting example of the effects of strong competition on a previously "safe" brand.

Camp Coffee: Coffee essences have slumped as the instant and total coffee markets have expanded. An old-fashioned image? Product taste out of tune with changed consumer tastes? Probably, but it is very likely that some of the lost market could be recaptured with the right revitalization policy.

Oxo: An example of a long-established, in a sense basically old-fashioned, product which has kept up to date by projecting an image acceptable to today's housewives and by extending usage with the introduction of Golden Oxo.

Cinema: With attendances down from 755m in 1958 to 215m in 1969 seems a ripe candidate for revitalization. Will never serve the old role of the cinema, but needs to be restructured in tune with today's new leisure needs. Possibly cinema complexes with other entertainment facilities as leisure centres.

Lifebuoy: A very old-fashioned soap which has held on to an important brand share by successfully updating its image.

Woolworths: The bazaar store ideally fitted the needs of the emerging working classes in the earlier part of this century. Changed spending power and attitudes to design and service in-store has not yet been fully reflected in modernization of Woolworth stores.

Harrods: The "Way In" concept is an interesting example of revitalization in updating image to appeal to young market without altering the traditional stability of appeal of the conventional Harrods store.

Aspro: The long-establishment of Aspro was threatened by the emergence if new analgesic products. The introduction of micro-fined Aspro was a revitalization tactic to modernize the brand's appeal.

One could go on citing cases of revitalization and of neglected revitalization; the potential for modernizing or revitalizing Tizer, Home and Colonial, Dunn's, Basildon Bond; the steps that have been taken to revitalize the bread market with Day Seals and Take "n" Bake, to modernize stationery retailing through Ryman Conran; to revitalize the shoe polish market with convenience products, and the welcome revitalization of British Rail with services like Inter City catering for changed transport needs.

Revitalization is not new in itself – only the approach to it I have outlined is new. And there are no guarantees of success in revitalization, any more than there are in new product development.

The revitalization programme described gives a more accurate diagnosis of the problems besetting products, and leads to more creative solutions for their interpretation into a revitalization plan – which can often be a less costly venture than the hunt for a new product.

17

PRICING IN
THE RETAIL BUSINESS

An examination of the way prices are set in retail outlets, by Professor André Gabor of Nottingham University's Consumer Study Group. Professor Gabor, who is also associated with the Department of Economics at Essex University and with Pricing Research Ltd., is an internationally recognized authority on pricing matters.

Retail pricing has two main aspects. With the exception of manufacturers who have their own retail outlets, the actual price at which a product is sold to the consumer is in the hands of the retail distributors, but the limits within which the latter can set their prices is, of course, still under the control of the manufacturers. In this article retail pricing will be discussed under these two main headings, not forgetting the special case of the store brands.

How do retailers price?

According to the February 1973 issue of the *Nielsen Researcher*, some 15 to 20 per cent of the failures of new consumer products can be attributed to the price/value factor. We have no data available to tell us how many retail establishments yield unsatisfactory financial results because of inappropriate pricing, but common experience suggests that the numbers are likely to be very substantial, year after year.

There was a time in the not too distant past when merchandisers considered price the least important item in the marketing mix, and in fact there was some truth in this while shortages rather than an abundance of goods dominated the market. But even later, for quite some years after the end of World War Two, it was still widely held that what mattered was to get the goods into the shops and that the best way of convincing the shopkeeper that the brand concerned would be a fast mover was to reveal to him the large extent of media advertising support planned.

Since then, the importance of point-of purchase factors in general and price in particular have received widespread recognition. This was not unconnected with another simultaneous development: the increased ascendancy of the large scale multiples and the shift of power it entailed.

The demise of resale price maintenance (which was as much the result of the introduction of the new American retailing techniques as the effect of the relevant legislation) means that pricing has become to a considerable extent the prerogative of the retail distributors. The shift of power has also moved profits down the line: large chains buy directly from the manufacturers and have not only appropriated the wholesaler's cut, but have also reduced the manufacturer's own prices, thereby benefiting both their customers and themselves. Yet, it is more the manufacturers than the retail distributors who have recognized the importance of the modern approach to pricing problems and who are making increasing use of pricing research to find the most promising prices for new and existing products.

Many distributors and especially the smaller ones do not seem to have any well thought out pricing system. This is hardly surprising if we consider that a similar lack of a definite attitude to price often occurs also higher up the line. A research team which investigated pricing in a number of the largest American manufacturing companies had to reach the conclusion that "It is not always evident that the price makers in the various big companies know that there is a policy, even if an inconsistent one."[1] Enquiries conducted in this country produced similar results and revealed in some cases also that the policy the executives of the

---

[1] Kaplan, A. D. H., Dirlam, J. B. and Lanzilotti, R. F., *Pricing in Big Business*, The Brookings Institution, Washington, D.C., 1958, p. 276.

firms concerned believed to be pursued by their own price setters had little to do with what actually happened in practice.[1]

This lack of an effective control of pricing is particularly evident in retail distribution. In the course of my own market research I have come across a number of instances where the prices displayed in the supermarkets were very different from those prescribed by the management, and the experience of other market researchers confirms my findings. Some of the discrepancies observed were due to deliberate departure from the policy of the management (a point which I will take up presently), but it is my impression that the bulk was simply the result of carelessness. The harm pricing mistakes can cause is far too great for complacency.

It has been alleged, and also supported by evidence, that some store managers are tempted to increase the profitability of their individual stores by not passing on to their customers the full extent of temporary price reductions. A few years ago Unilever sponsored an investigation of these practices and subsequently published the findings in a booklet circulated within the trade that bore the title *The money she might have spent*. It was shown there that not cutting the price by the full amount stipulated by the central management of the chain (often in conformity with the manufacturers' proposition) reduced both the sales of the item concerned and the profit that resulted from the promotion. My own view is that this issue requires further careful exploration, since the increase in the sale of the promoted item inevitably cuts into the turnover of the other brands sold by the same outlet in the same product field. Hence it is possible that overall profitability will be higher when the price reduction is, say, 2p rather than 3p.

Since retail establishments are of an extremely varied nature, it could hardly be expected that they would all follow an identical pricing policy, or that there should exist a single principle which would be ideal for all of them. In fact, the cheapest shop in town

[1] Pearce, I. F., "A Study in Price Policy," *Economica*, May 1966, pp. 114–27, Pearce, I. F. and Amey, L. R., "Price Policy with a Branded Product," *Review of Economic Studies*, 1956–57, pp. 49–60, Hague, D. C., *Pricing in Business*, George Allen and Unwin, London, 1971.

and the most expensive might be found equally successful. What is impossible is to be all things to all men: opposite extremes of business policy will not mix and hence consistency in pricing is an aim well worth pursuing.

Main pricing methods

Let us now look at the main methods of pricing in retail outlets and consider the pros and cons of each approach.

Secret price codes, intelligible to the staff only, were much in use in my early days, especially in the better-class shops. This practice, which seems to have largely if not entirely disappeared, was really that of individual pricing: it was left to the assistant to vary the price according to the estimate of the ability and willingness of the customer to pay. Even today, prices are not always prominently displayed in the shops that cater for the highest income groups, but the practice of adjusting the price to the customer is not now regarded as the best method for ensuring profitability in the long run.

Next, there is the fixed mark-up system, which consists of adding the same percentage to the cost of each item. It is much beloved by many small firms but was rightly described by the sales director of a large retailing organization as "the antithesis of good retail merchandising".[1] Indeed, in spite of its simplicity, there is nothing to commend it. Inevitably, it will lead to an inconsistent structure of retail prices, relatively overpricing some items and underpricing others. Any firm that clings to this practice in the face of intelligent competition is asking for trouble.

A more sophisticated version of the mark-up system is the one in which the actual percentage varies in proportion with the average length of time each type of product stays on the shelves. The price is thus related to the time for which capital is tied down and has much to commend itself. Provided the general level of prices and their structure are competitive in the eyes of the customers, this method is not inconsistent with the aim of securing

[1] May, P., "Retail Pricing", *Gazette of the John Lewis Partnership*, October 1959, p. 791.

FLOW DIAGRAM FOR REACTION TO COMPETITOR'S PRICE CUT

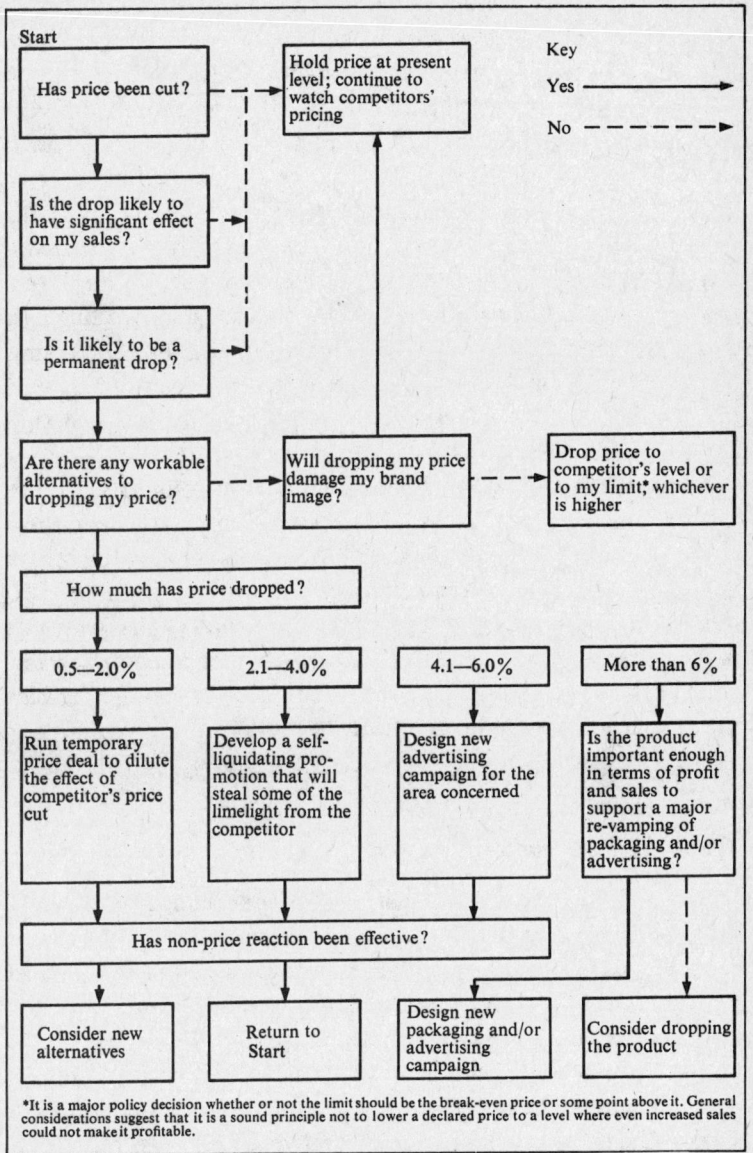

*It is a major policy decision whether or not the limit should be the break-even price or some point above it. General considerations suggest that it is a sound principle not to lower a declared price to a level where even increased sales could not make it profitable.

Redrawn, with modifications, from Philip Kotler, **Marketing Management** Prentice-Hall Inc, Englewood Cliffs, NJ,1967, Figure 15-4, p 379.

a favourable rate of return on the capital of the enterprise all the way round.

It hardly needs mention that in the case of perishables, fashion articles and goods in seasonal demand allowance has to be made for the loss through wastage and unsold remainders.

We now come to a pricing practice based on an entirely different idea; it was imported from the US and has been faithfully followed by several of the largest supermarket chains, with greatly varying success. Its essence is to maintain a general price level by having each day a few special bargains (or, at least, what give the customers the impression of special bargains) prominently displayed, while the prices of most of the other items are made to fluctuate around a central level. This is supposed to achieve three aims to give the impression of cheap prices in general, to attract bargain hunters and to discourage selective shopping. The last two aims are, of course, to some extent mutually exclusive!

I myself am somewhat doubtful about the soundness of this practice, expecially in view of the consistent success of those chains, notably Marks & Spencer's and Sainsbury's, which have deliberately opted for keeping prices as steady as possible in an inflationary period. Characteristically, Sainsbury's mark-up rate is of a much lower order than that of Marks & Spencer's, a fact which is well explained by the difference in turnover-rate between the product-mixes of the two firms.

What attracts customers to a store?

While it is certainly true that shops, like branded goods, have their image and this is what attracts or repels customers, I would contend that the extent to which the image can differ from reality is very limited, however much is being spent on promotion.

In connection with a large research project conducted by my research group a few years ago, we received both financial support and excellent facilities for pricing experiments in the supermarkets of the Greater Nottingham Co-operative Society. In return, we offered the Society the use of the survey for the exploration of the main aspects of its image in the eyes of its customers by comparison with those of other supermarket chains in the area.

The results, which were subsequently published,[1] surprised the Society's management: it was revealed that some of the factors they considered important were not rated highly by their customers. Equally interesting, the price image of its stores was relatively unfavourable, contrary to the Society's intended policy.

The fact that such elements as cleanliness, quick service, pleasant atmosphere were not rated high on the subjective scales does not necessarily mean that customers attach little importance to them. The proper interpretation is rather that since the degree of cleanliness, for example, which they expect can be found in many other stores, it is not a special attraction. And as far as the price image was concerned, a subsequent price-comparison survey clearly indicated that the management was right in believing that its pricing was competitive, insofar as the average level of its prices compared favourably with that of its competitors, yet the structure of its prices prevented a heavy proportion of its customers from taking this view.

While space does not permit further details of this enquiry as laid out in the published report, I should like to say that they clearly indicate how useful it can be to explore the image of a store or chain. Even a small survey can throw up extremely important aspects that might not have come otherwise to the notice of the management.

The policy of fluctuating prices has led to an additional practice of rather doubtful value. When the store next door operates a price promotion with a particular brand, some retailers respond by temporarily removing the same brand from their shelves.

Finally, a few words about the pricing of store brands. It seems to me that there are three clearly distinguishable principles that can easily be identified with the firms that practise them. First, there is the Fortnum & Mason–Harrods principle: "If we put our name on a product, this means that it is the finest in existence

[1] Gabor, A. and Sowter, A. P., "The Customers' Views" and "How Competitive is the Co-op?," *Co-operative Management and Marketing,* 1970 and 1971.

and you must expect to pay for it accordingly". Next, we have the Marks & Spencer's–Sainsbury's–Boots principle: "We give honest value for money; our product is at least equal in quality to that of our competitors, and if our price is not below the competitive level, the customer will find that there is more in the pack." Lastly, there is the cheapjack principle, and here I will refrain from naming its practitioners: "Our prices are the lowest, so you should not complain if the goods are not quite up to the standard of the best." The way the market is moving, I can see a much brighter future for the first two policies than for the third.

How should manufacturers price?

Since I have already mentioned the fact that many manufacturers do not seem to pursue any recognizable pricing policy, I will not try to expose further their current pricing practices but concentrate on the methods which I believe are most likely to be conducive to success.

For new products it is convenient to use the concepts introduced by Joel Dean:[1] skimming price and penetration price are the policies between which the manufacturer must choose. The former is particularly suited for real novelties and suggests that any such product should be introduced at the top end of the market at a price which could well be a multiple of the current production cost. This is calculated to provide an early contribution to development expenses and to keep the demand at a level which a relatively small and perhaps even partly experimental plant could satisfy. The high price will also impart prestige to the product. Later, as the production facilities are expanded, price may be reduced without impairing profitability, and the lower price will help to discourage potential competition. Needless to say a skimming price policy can only reduce risks; it cannot eliminate them. It paid off with Nylon hoisery but led to a very substantial loss (reported to be around $80m) in the case of Corfam.

[1] Dean, J., *Managerial Economics,* Prentice-Hall, Englewood Cliffs, N. Jersey, 1951; "Pricing Policies for New Products," *Harvard Business Review*, November/December, 1950; "Pricing a New Product," *The Controller*, April 1965.

Most of the new products that come to the market are not real novelties but merely new brands that have to find their place in an established market. However loudly it is proclaimed that the new brand of, say, toothpaste, gives you a superior sparkle and a cast-iron ring of confidence, the customer will judge it as yet another toothpaste which might be given a try if the marketing mix, of which the 'price is a highly important component, appears to be right. Hence a penetration price (also called "volume-based price") is indicated right from the start.

Test marketing might be used to explore the reactions of the customers, but since it is not the first purchase but the repurchase rate that counts, it can take quite a long time and could be a rather expensive way of finding out that the new brand is a failure.

I am certainly not against marketing experiments of the right kind, but I do not consider it the best approach to the problem. What does appear to be a far more promising method is essentially similar to that practised by firms like Marks & Spencer: find the price first, then find out what customers would expect at that price, see if you can develop it so that it should be profitable, then pre-test to find out if your judgement was a fair guess of what your potential customers think, and do your test marketing only at this stage. Marks & Spencer uses empathy rather than a structured approach, and of course if you have the gift of finding out what your customers think simply by a bit of introspection, you need neither consultants nor market research. For those who are not so gifted, there exists a well-developed and validated method that I will briefly outline here. It has been described in detail elsewhere.[1]

It is based on the buy-response curve, obtained by interviewing an appropriate sample of respondents, each of whom is asked if he (or she) would buy the product in question at various prices which are presented in a randomized order. The buy response-curve shows the percentage of customers interested at each of the prices. This, coupled with the distribution of prices paid by the

[1] Gabor, A. and Granger, C. W. J., "The Pricing of New Products," *Scientific Business*, August, 1965; Gabor, A., "New Product Pricing," *Marketing*, February 1971.

subjects for their last purchases, will indicate the prospects of the proposed new product according to the price at which it will be marketed.[1]

A related method is available to help in the repricing of existing brands. The predictor obtained will show the relationship between price differences and relative market shares of the competing brands.[2]

These techniques have been tested in a number of shop trials and have been in use over the years by several leading companies. While the methods themselves are simple, their application and the interpretation of the results require expert handling. A special case is that of product line pricing, particularly the price structure of a line consisting of different pack sizes of the same brand.[3]

Finally, it should be realized that a price which is most advantageous under present conditions might require quick adjustment if there is a change in the situation, for example if one of the main competitors cuts his price. It is highly advisable to develop in advance a strategy for such purposes, the essence of which can be embodied in a decision tree, of the kind shown opposite.

[1] Gabor A. and Granger, C. W. J., "Price as an Indicator of quality," *Economica*, 1966, pp. 43–70; "The Attitude of the Consumer to Price," *Pricing Strategy* (Taylor, B. and Wills, G. eds.), Staples Press, London, 1969, pp. 132–51.

[2] Sowter, A. P. Gabor, A. and Granger, C. W. J., "The Influence of Price Differences on Brand Shares and Switching," *British Journal of Marketing*, Winter 1960, pp. 223–30; "Real and Hypothetical Shop Situations in Market Research," *Journal of Marketing Research*, August 1970, pp. 355–59; "The Effect of Price on Choice," *Applied Economics*, 1971 (3), pp. 167–81.

[3] Granger, C. W. J. and Billson, A., "Consumers' Attitudes Towards Package Size and Price," *Journal of Marketing Research*, August 1972, pp. 239–48.

18

APPLYING MARKET SEGMENTATION ON A GLOBAL SCALE

Simon Majaro, author of this article, is a partner in Urwick Orr, a director of Strategic Management Learning and a faculty member of the Centre d'Etudes Industrielles where he was formerly head of the marketing department.

Selling abroad is not synonymous with international marketing. It is not always appreciated that there is a big difference between companies that syphon off excess home production into foreign markets and companies that start *ab initio* exploring world markets as part of their overall marketing strategy. The former start at home and when they feel sufficiently established they seek opportunities abroad. The latter systematically seeks world-wide markets and try to derive profits from satisfying their respective needs.

The export-oriented company tries to maximise its profits through increased sales abroad and the resultant reduction in the production unit costs. The international marketer looks at the world as one market with a host of marketing opportunities; he aims to satisfy those which he considers would yield the best results for his firm. In other words he applies the market segmentation theory on a global scale.

Market segmentation normally means the identification of a group of people inside a market who share a common need. The international marketer can be said to apply the same principle. He tries to identify meaningful buyer groups throughout the world and then gears his marketing effort towards the fulfilment of their needs. The difference between the international marketer and his domestic counterpart in this respect is mainly a matter of dimension. His segments, if he has managed to identify them, are multinational.

This, of course, presupposes that the international marketing man believes that the marketing concept can be applied to world markets. And we all know that the marketing concept, in spite of its persuasive appeal, is still causing problems on the domestic front. So what chance can it possibly stand in world markets?

Few companies would challenge the logic behind the marketing concept. We all believe that the modern firm should start its marketing process with its customers – existing and potential; it should seek to attain profits through the creation of customer satisfaction; and it should achieve this objective through an integrated marketing programme. To the average marketing man this almost sounds trite. But although the concept earns much lip-service there are few European companies which have fully adopted the marketing concept with all its implications and rigours. It is a sad reflection on modern managers that even the most dedicated converts to the marketing concept often recoil from the discipline which its adoption implies.

"We introduced the marketing concept into our company over five years ago," an enlightened chairman of a large international company told the writer recently. "Unfortunately the recession in the United States has forced us to keep many useless products in our range. Our machines would be half idle if we decided to discontinue them." For this chairman the marketing concept is a luxury that can only be indulged in when the country and the world are enjoying a period of prosperity!

A still more succinct example is a company which recently adopted, with suitable fanfare, the marketing concept as a way of life. Considerable effort was invested in explaining the notion to company personnel. The call to devote everybody's attention to market needs and gear the marketing task towards the satisfaction of consumer wants was proclaimed as an irrevocable corporate edict. Within a few days of the great proclamation a high pressure note from the top executives was circulated among all employees: "We have recently installed the fastest and most modern mill in our Dutch plant, but we have very little work for this new equipment. It is essential that we find orders quickly, so as to keep the factory busy. Anybody in the company who comes up with ideas which lead to the plant being profitably occupied will be awarded £10 worth of premium bonds."

What a tragic epitaph to a valiant attempt to turn a company into a marketing oriented enterprise!

These are examples from domestic companies that may have small interests abroad. What about the firm that is trying to go truly international or at least market its products internationally? The marketing concept calls for an integrated process for creating customer satisfaction at a profit to the company. Is it possible to satisfy customers on a world-wide scale? This needs a closer exploration.

Satisfying the customer implies that the total marketing mix should be formulated so as to provide the consumer with the utilities of form, time and place which he is seeking to obtain. In fact, every ingredient of the marketing mix should be designed so as to fulfil the consumer needs. First the product has to meet his requirements. When we talk about the product we include all the peripheral utilities such as packaging, branding, instructions for use, after-sale service and many other attributes. To use Theodore Levitt's terminology we include all the "product augmentation" ingredients. Then we have to ensure that the price, promotion, distribution policies and sales direction are planned so as to meet the consumer's desires. Each of these ingredients adds to the total satisfaction. At the same time the marketing planner has to contend with the environmental and institutional factors operating in the market place.

The international marketer has the same problem but multiplied by the number of markets he aims to satisfy. The mind boggles at the number of permutations that he has to evolve or select from. To try to develop all the relevant "mixes" from one central planning point is enough to discourage the bravest marketing men. After all, there will not only be a need to modify the product to conform with certain national standards but more often than not there will be further pressures inside the countries to develop additional modifications. Similarly, pricing policies may differ from country to country; distribution policies will need to be altered in the light of available channels; promotion strategies reconsidered in the absence of suitable media. To try to perform a meaningful job from a central vantage point is a sisyphean task.

It is not surprising, therefore, that the average international marketer takes the easy way out by abdicating the marketing planning task to local management throughout the world markets. This is not a criticism of such a policy – on the face of it there is little or no alternative. It is difficult to see how an international marketer could undertake to determine the optimum "mix" for every market from a centralised position. On the other hand the belief is commonly held nowadays that it is only through a certain amount of centralized control and/or co-ordination, that the total marketing effort can yield maximum results from world markets. It is perhaps with this philosophy in mind that Unilever decided a few years ago to create the function of world co-ordinators for a few of its major product groups.

It is worth considering to what extent the concept of market segmentation, as applied to world markets, can come to the rescue. On the face of it the term "segmentation" appears to be the antithesis of "international" marketing. The former's purpose is to deal with micro-markets, the latter with macro-markets. Segmentation refers to sub-markets; internationalization to global markets. The contradiction is, however, only a matter of dimension and not of concept. Whether we talk about segments of a domestic market or large chunks of an international market we want to satisfy a specific target-group. The aim to satisfy a target-group implies that the marketer has determined who his consumer is. This is the essence of marketing, both domestic and international. It is normally agreed that no product and no marketing mix can satisfy everybody at the same time.

The modern marketer searches for broad classes of buyers who differ in product interests or marketing susceptibilities. He can segment his market on a host of different bases. He can select socio-economic variables; geographic areas; usage rate; end use; sensitivity to price, quality or aesthetic values, etc. The international marketer can also segment his markets. Political borders are not necessarily the best way to draw a distinction among target groups. Experienced marketers will be the first to admit that the Dutch consumer has a lot more in common with the German buyer than with the French-speaking Belgian although the Dutch and the Belgians are supposed to belong to the closely-knit Benelux unit. Furthermore the inhabitant of Geneva often displays consumer habits which are much nearer to those of the Frenchman than those of the Swiss from Zurich. They both live in the same country, but can easily be attached to identifiable non-Swiss target groups.

In the UK we are fortunate in having the IPA system which provides us with a socio-economic basis for segmenting our market. This basis encapsulates a combination of income occupation and social status. These are expressed on a scale of six grades: A, B, C1, C2, D and E. Most marketing men find it a convenient tool for segmenting markets and appraising opportunities. The international marketer is less fortunate. He has to evolve his own basis for segmenting his global market. Indeed, establishing the most appropriate basis for dividing the world market into suitable and meaningful segments is one of his major tasks.

It is worth reviewing at this point the various strategies which the marketing man can adopt. The strategy selected for a specific situation normally depends on whether a segmentation policy has been adopted or not. The firm may choose one of the following: *undifferentiated marketing; differentiated marketing* and *concentrated marketing*. In the first instance it places on the market one product and tries to draw as many consumers as possible with one uniform marketing mix. In the second case it modifies the product and the "mix" to appeal specifically to each segment. In the third instance it isolates a small number of promising segments and it concentrates the total effort on these limited sub-markets.

Normally a domestic company that decides to export part of its production tends to use an undifferentiated marketing strategy. The thinking here is that the extra sales abroad should be treated as "gravy" and therefore the less one indulges product modification or manipulation of the "mix", the better. It has been aptly suggested that undifferentiated marketing is the counterpart of standardisation and mass-production in manufacturing.

At the other extreme we have the company that wishes to satisfy as many consumers in its world markets as possible. It resorts to a differentiated marketing strategy. It has identified a host of needs and it has embarked on the gargantuan and costly task of attempting to gear the product, the promotion activity, the distribution policy, the price and the sales effort to each country or each sub-market. This inevitably leads sooner of later, to each sub-market becoming a self-contained and highly decentralised marketing entity. The job of co-ordinating the activities of all these sub-markets becomes very tenuous.

It is normally true to say that differentiated marketing, whether it is applied within a domestic market or is extended to world markets, is sales-oriented rather than profit-oriented. If Coca-Cola decided to adjust all the ingredients of the marketing mix to every sub-market, it would soon find itself producing scores of flavours in dozens of different bottles or packs; the advertising effort would differ enormously from country to country; the pricing policy would be in a state of disarray and the distribution strategy would get totally out of hand. Coca-Cola would probably sell more but at what extra cost? In fact the product would cease to be Coca-Cola; it would become a host of products – each market would have a specially designed and bottled beverage produced and marketed by a company called Coca-Cola.

The third strategy mentioned above was concentrated marketing. The first two strategies differentiated and undifferentiated, imply that the marketer goes after the whole market. Whilst the undifferentiated strategy aims at maximum sales with one single "mix", the differentiated strategy is willing to make changes in the product and the "mix" to satisfy different requirements. The concentrated marketing, on the other hand, implies that the firm goes after a small share of a large market. Instead of spreading itself thinly in many parts of the world it decides to concentrate its forces on a few clearly defined areas. The company tries to

Table 1

COUNTRY: ABC
PRODUCT: XYZ (DOMESTIC APPLIANCE)

	ELEMENTS OF THE MARKETING MIX				
	PRODUCT	PRICE	DISTRIBUTION	PROMOTION	SELLING
I. THE ENVIRONMENT					
II. CULTURAL FACTORS					
III. THE CONSUMER					
IV. ECONOMIC DEVELOPMENT					
V. INDUSTRIAL DEVELOPMENT					
VI. COMPETITIVE TRENDS					
VII. LEGAL CONSTRAINTS	Strict Electrical Standards	Anti-Cartel Law Retail Price Maintenance Allowed	Retail Price Maintenance. Contracts with Agents Difficult to Terminate.	Strong Trade Mark Laws. Trade Description Act. Restriction on Advert Expenditure.	No Restrictions. Trade Description Regulations.
VIII. MARKETING INSTITUTIONS					
IX. OTHER FACTORS					

GENERAL REMARKS:

achieve a strong position in these countries or sub-markets where it has established its competence to satisfy the local consumers with a limited cluster of highly standardized products and marketing mixes. Every international marketer who has ever experienced the agonies of differentiation on a global scale would admit that standardization of marketing strategies is his deeply-felt ambition. However, standardization is a highly skilful job. It implies that the marketing company has done its homework properly and has pinpointed clearly its target areas throughout the world. An example of successful concentrated strategy based on maximum product and marketing standardization, is the Volkswagen story.

Concentrated marketing implies that the company has opted to tie its future growth to well-defined world sub-markets with a standardized marketing mix or a small number of such mixes. Of course this carries some risks. Competitors may decide to carve a slice of the market for themselves and if the "concentrating" company has placed all its eggs in one basket, a drop in the market may mean a disastrous drop in sales and profits. However, most companies that have adopted a concentrated strategy in their world markets have found that the benefits far outweigh the risks. These companies have discovered that the main benefits have included greater effectiveness in marketing, reduced costs, improved planning and easier control.

Concentrated marketing at the multinational level, as already implied, means that the marketer should be able to attain a measure of standardization of his product and the marketing mix. If he fails to achieve this objective it is often due to the fact that he has not managed to assemble all the information about his international markets. Knowledge of one's markets is a vital ingredient in an effective performance of the marketing task. This becomes even more important in international marketing. Inadequate knowledge of international markets usually leads to the abdication of marketing decisions to local management and the latter invariably clamour for changes in the product and the "mix". This makes the whole concept of standardization impossible. The most important message for the international marketer is that to be able to standardize his product, promotional material, distribution and sales policies he must possess and be able to interpret a wealth of data about each one of his markets. The effort is great but the benefits can be greater. Standardization followed by a policy of concentrated marketing or at the most a partially differentiated marketing carry sufficient benefits in terms of cost savings and general effectiveness to justify the effort.

It was suggested with some emphasis that the essential input that the international marketer needs to possess is comprehensive data about the various countries in which the firm seeks its fortunes. The data thus collected should provide information about the environment, cultural background, the consumer and his habits, economic development, industrial development, competitive trends, legal constraints, available marketing institutions and any other relevant data. Each one of these factors may have an important bearing on the way the various ingredients of the marketing mix will be approached. Thus, for example, a brief study of one market may show that the advertising media available in one country are incompatible with media considered appropriate in other countries. Similarly a study of marketing institutions in a country may reveal that the wholesalers' structure is weak as compared to the position in neighbouring countries. This means that a serious constraint has been detected which may preclude any hope of standardisation in relation to a very important element of the "mix". This should be documented and the difficulty "stored" for subsequent adjudication.

Another situation that a thorough study may reveal is that the legal system imposes awkward limitations on the freedom to determine a company's pricing decisions. Alternatively the contractual obligations of having exclusive agents may be too onerous in certain territories.

The international marketer should proceed on a systematic and comprehensive data-collecting procedure about each market. Until this process is completed it is futile for any marketer to think that he is in the position of developing strategies in relation to his world markets.

Table 1 illustrates a simple matrix which the international marketer can use in documenting his basic information about each

Table 2

Bench-mark Territory:	ELEMENTS OF THE MARKETING MIX				
	PRODUCTS	PRICE	DISTRIBUTION	PROMOTION	SALES MANAGEMENT
	0 1 2 3 4 5 6 7 8 9 10	0 1 2 3 4 5 6 7 8 9 10	0 1 2 3 4 5 6 7 8 9 10	0 1 2 3 4 5 6 7 8 9 10	0 1 2 3 4 5 6 7 8 9 10
e.g. Germany	ns s	ns s	ns s	ns s	ns s
France					
Holland					
Belgium					
Italy					
U.K.					
Switzerland					
Spain					
Portugal					

market. When the matrix is conscientiously completed he will possess a market profile. He should repeat the exercise in relation to every market. The top row lists the ingredients of the marketing mix. The left column enumerates the major factors that influence the kind of "mix" which can be formulated for the specific market in question. The international planner should attempt to complete every cell on this matrix except those which appear irrelevant to the better understanding of the market and its needs.

The cells on the "Legal Constraints" row were completed to illustrate the type of information that should be sought.

No effort should be spared in ensuring that the information collected is complete and that the details have been validated through personal investigations or the use of reliable outside sources. The study may lead to major and long-term decisions being taken and it is therefore vital that the information assembled is sound. It pays to perform this task thoroughly and efficiently. The matrix is only meant as a summary sheet and naturally all the supporting evidence and details should be close at hand.

When the study and the summary work is completed the international marketer should be in possession of market profiles on all the markets he wants to analyse. The profile as documented on the matrix form is a thumb-nail sketch of each market. The material can now be used to identify those markets which lend themselves to a standardization approach and those which do not. Alternatively it should now be possible to isolate a cluster of markets capable of being handled in a homogeneous way thus reducing the marketing "mixes" to a manageable number. In other words we should find ourselves in the position of selecting one of two strategies. In the first place we could seek a concentrated strategy in relation to a cluster of markets and devote all our energy towards the full exploitation of this cluster of markets. In the second place we can adopt a limited differentiated policy with a small but manageable number of "mixes" with each mix applied to a defined cluster of markets or regions. The thing to avoid in international marketing is a limitless differentiated policy which is tantamount to a total fragmentation of effort with a virtual abandonment of control to "local" management. In this latter case international marketing ceases to be international; it becomes a free-for-all under one flag.

An aid to clear thinking on the question of standardization of the international marketing process is shown in Table II.

The idea behind this table is the attempt to force oneself to extract some conclusions from the market profiles so laboriously assembled. On this table one lists all the countries that the company wishes to include in its international plan. At the top of the list one places the country which one has selected as the basic "bench mark" territory Normally the bench mark will either be the home country of the manufacturer or the country which one has selected as the most promising market.

Once again the top row shows the various elements of the marketing mix; the left column lists the countries under observation. Each element of the mix has a scale, in relation to each country, ranging from 0 to 10. "0" implies that there is no hope of standardization in relation to the bench mark territory and the appropriate element of the "mix". "10" means that standardization is perfectly feasible. In between one can insert an X at the point which seems to the international analyst as the most appropriate. Inevitably a certain amount of subjective judgement is bound to creep into this exercise. However, such subjective judgement is at least based on a thorough knowledge of the facts. To overcome any risk of excessive subjectivity it is possible to use a committee of managers with each member inserting his personal perception of the situation on the grid. An average of the various opinions expressed on the grid will carry the weight of a "jury of executive opinion" approach.

Interesting results emerge from this exercise. One can discern almost at a glance those markets that enjoy some homogeneity with the "bench mark" country or territory and those that do not. If one decides in advance that any point on the grid higher than "7" augurs well for standardization purposes useful outputs can be derived from a brief glance at the table.

Table II shows that in relation to a specific product (a domestic appliance) all the ingredients of the "mix" were over "7" in Germany, Holland, Belgium and Switzerland. In other words we have at least established that in these four countries we can operate, in relation to the product under study, with a standard product and marketing strategy. No doubt if we decided to differentiate our marketing strategy among these countries we should achieve still higher sales but the cost is not justified in the light of our findings. We are now in the position of obtaining maximum mileage from a standardized "mix".

This is a good start. We have identified a cluster of markets which will favourably respond to a "marketing package". We can now repeat the exercise in order to identify another cluster of markets which will respond to a second standardized "package" and so on. The aim is clearly established – we wish to reduce the number of "mixes" to a small and manageable and homogeneously standard marketing strategy. If pursued with imagination and clear perception of the differences among markets it can yield considerable benefits to the marketing company. The wastefulness of over-differentiation and the constraining effect of non-differentiation can be avoided. Moreover, the international marketer's "golden fleece", viz. the implementation of the "International Marketing Concept", may become more easily attainable.

19
MOTIVATING
OVERSEAS AGENTS

International salesmanship is not, in principle, any different from selling at home. What is overlooked is that every market is someone else's home market; customers do not see themselves as export buyers. By Sydney Paulden.

This article is from a book by BBC Publications. Called Hardy Heating International – Exporting in practice, *it accompanied a series of ten TV programmes.*

Hardy Heating is a company invented originally at BBC for the purpose of illustrating an earlier series on Management Accountancy. The author of the new book, Sydney Paulden, was given the brief to launch Hardy Heating into export markets. He found that BBC, like the majority of UK manufacturers, had created the company with no thought of possible future entry into international marketing, so it had all the defects which face firms suddenly needing to expand their horizons.

Hardy Heating's products were unsuitable, for technical reasons, for a large proportion of the world's markets. Its staff had no experience of overseas selling, of international transport organization or of export documentation.

The book leads Hardy Heating step-by-step into export marketing, from desk research to on-the-spot investigation of local potential; from the first Board discussion on the advisability of entering foreign markets, to later problems of liquidity due to expanding markets.

BBC TV producer Paul Ellis, who is responsible for the whole project, chose to put the spotlight on export marketing because he discovered that exporting was a side of business which demanded its own skills and its own specialist knowhow. He found, at the same time, that Britain was ludicrously short of the right facilities for training executives or students at any level. BBC TV's Further Education series, with this book and the ten programmes, aimed to contribute something towards meeting the requirement for greater study of all aspects of exporting – market research, distribution, personnel, finance, licensing, costing, quoting and documentation.

Each chapter of the book, and each TV programme, had an introductory statement of the principles involved (as in this extract from "International Salesmanship"). followed by a dramatized case study based on the experiences of the Hardy Heating Company. Though fictitious, the details of each case had been researched to make them as closely realistic as possible. Now read on.

Whether the representative in a foreign market is an agent acting on commission, or whether he is a sole distributor buying for resale at a profit, the exporter must always regard the market as his own, not that of the local man. Agents can become inefficient or inactive; they can retire or die; they can withdraw from the agreement in order to take some other product line. The exporter must always feel himself responsible for the long-term welfare of each of his markets. To do this he has to work closely with his representative to ensure that his products, and his company image, are introduced in the most effective way, and he has to keep himself so well informed about progress, or lack of it, that he is able to take remedial action if things go wrong. Very few exporters can claim with any honesty that they have been quick enough off the mark when there has been a need to sack an agency. Normally, through neglect and pressure of work, such action is only taken long after a market has gone bad, making all the more difficult the task of re-entry.

One of the major differences between marketing abroad and marketing at home is the feeling of isolation which can grow in the consciousness of a foreign representative. It is apt to happen even with sales reps stationed in Plymouth or Dundee who sell on behalf of manufacturers in Manchester or Birmingham, and this sentiment is all the more a danger if a British firm is dependent upon agents in Melbourne, Mexico City or Milan.

If sales are below expectations in a foreign market, there are three possible lines of action, all of which require up-to-date information to be effective. The exporter can:

1. revise targets, because of obvious miscalculations;
2. motivate the agent (if investigations show he could really do better);
3. change the agent (if he is seen to be incapable of exploiting the potential).

In 9 out of 10 cases, the first line is taken without any serious investigation of market conditions, competitors' progress or product acceptance. It is simply the easiest course to take from afar. International salesmanship is not, in principle, any different from salesmanship on the domestic market. After all, a thing which is often overlooked is that the export market is someone else's home market, and the end customers do not regard themselves as export buyers, but just as customers. It is in detail that export marketing differs, for there are the complications of different customs, different available channels of distribution, and distance. Within each market the exporter and his agent should be prepared to invest the time and money which are shown to be essential to reach maximum market penetration. It is astonishing how many manufacturers automatically allow a tiny proportion of their annual promotional budget to cover scores of foreign markets and then express severe disappointment with their export sales department because their world market share is not impressive.

As far as the effectiveness of direct advertising is concerned, this varies a good deal from market to market. There are also different opinions as to the advisability of controlling advertising from the exporter's head office or whether it is something which should be left to the discretion of local representatives. Perhaps the best system is a "synthesis", not a "compromise", of these two approaches. The exporter should be in a position to approve the advertising approach, retaining responsibility for the image being created for his products internationally. However, the agent and his local specialists (advertising agency) should be able to handle the creative side of advertising and should be responsible for selection of the best media. They should know better than the exporter what sort of message is most effective on their own market, assuming that the correct market segment is being aimed at, according to the marketing plan agreed with the principal.

This brings up the controversial question of: "Who pays for the local advertising?" Long experience on the part of scores of exporters who have been interviewed stresses the following definite truths:

1. If it is left to the agent to finance his own advertising, then he will tend to give it the minimum thought and spend the minimum money. Agents generally, the world over, regard advertising on their own account to be sheer loss of profits. This is true, also, even if a bigger discount or commission is granted for the express purpose of advertising promotion.

2. If the exporter finances local promotion, then the agent will tend to encourage spending to the point of wastefulness, with a minimum of thought and a maximum amount of money.

3. If the exporter controls advertising without local participation in planning or creative work, then he has every chance of taking the wrong tack and missing the target.

4. If the agent is responsible for planning a promotional campaign for the year to come; for explaining and selling this campaign to his principal; and if the agent is willing to back his judgement with 50 per cent of his own investment; then the exporter is very likely to be getting good value for the remaining 50 per cent which he covers.

Just as it is advisable to arrange for the agent to invest some of his own cash in advertising, so it is advisable to get him to invest some of his own time and effort in producing sales literature, technical manuals and catalogues. People everywhere tend to think of printed matter as "handouts" and "bumph", ignoring the fact that (a) it costs money to produce, and (b) it can serve a useful function if properly directed. Masses of printed brochures do nothing more than collect dust on the shelves of overseas agents who have made no plans to distribute them and who think they have nothing to lose by their waste.

At the same time, with export sales material, there is the added problem of local languages and terminology and local prices, which differ from those of the home market. Consequently, the way to ensure that the material is tailored exactly for the market, and that it is used effectively after delivery, is to oblige the agent to contribute to its production. A simple method is to produce the basic design and illustrations in bulk and then receive the texts and prices from each agent for printing into the requisite spaces. The agent can then purchase the final product from the exporter at a higher subsidized price. Having written the text and bought the brochures, the agent will be reasonable in the quantities he orders and will give some thought to their proper application.

It can be very damaging to a product's image if the accompanying literature (instructions for use, technical specifications etc.) is inaccurate, outmoded or bizarre in its phraseology. It can ruin any image of quality and reliability or it might stress the "foreignness" which the agent would prefer to keep in the background. The only way to avoid these undesirable connotations is for the local native-born representative to provide the texts. For example, there are big differences even between the Spanish spoken in one country of Latin America and the next, and they all differ from that spoken in Spain. Many countries are bilingual, requiring duplicated texts (e.g. Finland, Belgium, Switzerland – trilingual – South Africa and Hong Kong).

Films are a means of aiding a sales effort and have special relevance to foreign markets. Distance is often a hindrance to the creation of a company image in a short time, for companies well known at home can be completely unknown abroad, and it is not so easy to invite prospective customers to look over the plant or inspect a nearby successful installation or swanky showroom. Short films ("short" is the keyword!) can convey the size of the firm or any special aspect worth stressing (quality control, reliability, spares, stocks) in a speedy and memorable fashion.

Give-aways or premium gifts are more useful in some markets than direct advertising. In many parts of the world, in addition to the standard means of promotion, business gifts are an essential part of the business relationship procedure. The Middle East, Japan, parts of East Europe, and African territories frequently regard an exchange of gifts as a courteous way of cementing a friendship. It is all the more valuable if the gift can have some link with the products being marketed. Obvious examples are car key rings with petrol, ashtrays with cigarettes. A common practice is to have useful items such as cigarette lighters or tiepins engraved with the firm's logo or emblem. The local agent must be able to advise on these items, for lack of know-how can cause embarrassment. You might be thinking of miniature bottles of whisky for countries where religion forbids alcohol. Never get involved with emblems representing local flags without the most scrupulous checking. Not all folk like to see their flags put to commercial usage; and not all populations support the existing regimes.

Expanding from business gifts, one can bring in the question of actual bribery. This does play a part in business deals in an unfortunately large number of countries. The local agent will be fully conversant with its role and should put his principal entirely in the picture as to its nature, size and necessity, but it is up to the company to use its own conscience when making decisions as to its employment. At least, the exporter cannot ignore its existence and the Boards of exporting companies ought to give guidance to the salesmen in the field as to how the problem should be tackled.

But the most effective of all sales aids is the personal co-operation between exporter and agent and the only way to keep this active and healthy is to ensure frequent meetings in person – mainly through visits to the market area by the manufacturer's staff but also through invitations to the agent to visit the head office and factory in the home base. The personal meeting provides many benefits:

1. Prevention of friction through misunderstandings.
2. Re-enthusing of local agent, maintenance of his interest.
3. Feedback of market information to the principal.
4. Generation of actual business resulting from appointments with clients.

5. Completion of specific points of business on agenda.

This latter item, the agenda, rarely receives the attention it deserves. The two most common reasons for an overseas sales trip are:

1. Regular, routine call (annual, six-montly, biennial?).
2. Overcome emergency problem (collapse of market, hysterically unhappy customer, default of major payment).

This second reason rarely contributes to future smooth-running of marketing and often the first reason leaves the agent wondering why the principal's representative came at all. The rep may have collected orders, but they are likely to have been saved up for his visit by the agent, in the way that contracts are always signed with a great fanfare at exhibitions (contracts which have been hanging fire for weeks).

Visiting salesman (at home as well as abroad) should attempt to give constructive, positive objectives to their trips, objectives which take the marketing strategy a step further for everyone's obvious benefit. A few examples might be:

1. Maintenance of bigger local stocks to combat competition.
2. Switch of emphasis to larger unit sales, reducing sales costs and delivery costs.
3. Simplification of documentation and reporting.
4. The consideration of assembling locally a proportion of a product, in order to reduce import tariffs on the finished article.
5. Analysis of outlets, compared with market successes in other countries.
6. Special promotion schemes, such as exhibitions, invitation, to entertain important clients on trip back to factory; collaboration with local supermarket group.

If the export salesman has other duties (being, for example, the company sales director, or export manager with responsibility for several markets). the chances are that whilst he is away there will be a backlog of work piling up on his desk, ready to overface him on his return. He is normally thrown into the office problems to the extent that he is not capable of tying up the scores of loose ends which are inevitable with an overseas tour. He has promises to keep for agents and clients; reports to make for various departments in the company to complete new agreed procedures; action to take on quotations, revisions, sales material, order chasing and so on; but these tend to be neglected under the home-coming pressure and so a great deal of the good work achieved by an expensive trip is allowed to ebb away. The export salesman is met with double the normal work at exactly the moment when he is drained of energy and mental power by the exigencies of the travel, the changes of climate, food and time. The wise company management will, as a standard thing, allow the export salesman to recuperate at home (where other problems are bound to have accumulated such as bills, education queries, neglected gardens) for a couple of days, perhaps with the condition that he should then return to work with clarified reports and recommended lines of action. The business manager should give his team the same attention that the football manager deems essential for *his* team.

On the subject of titles never forget that . . . a title is also a tool. If our salesman is a vice-president and yours is a sales rep and both are in a waiting room, guess who gets in first and gets the most attention.

This point is all the more important in relation to selling in overseas territories, where many special courtesies are *de rigeur* for senior foreign visitors. A better title increases the salesman's chances immediately, and reflects well upon the local agent who is seen to be graced by the presence of someone with authority from the principal company. In areas where the state gets involved in purchasing (and these are the sources of so many of day's giant orders), then diplomatic protocol is brought to bear, with a Minister meeting the company chairman, a junior minister host to the sales director and the third-clerk-on-the-left-as-you-go-in appointed to give the bum's rush to the technical sales representative.

Coupled with the title importance is the question of daily expenses. Small allowances bring small orders from lowly contacts. If the agent is ashamed to give his colleague's hotel address to the client, then the colleague is in the wrong hotel! Just think of the different treatment a foreign visitor to your company is likely to get if you are asked to meet him for lunch at the Dorchester compared with a whisky from a toothbrush glass in a small "businessman's hotel". As the export visitor is hundreds of thousands of miles away from his company, his status and the image of his firm can only be measured by the yardstick of his hotel, his dinner entertainments, the speed with which he gets information by spending money on telephone calls to head office, on taxis and on hired cars. Cut these down and you cut down your image and your chances of making the right impression on agent and client.

20

SETTING UP FOR SELLING

When marketing in Continental Europe, agents and distributors may be the best way of starting. But only with a sales force of your own on the spot can you really claim that your overseas markets are no longer in a "different" category from home sales. By Stephen Ward.

Tariffs and the Channel are not the only roadblocks on the highway to Europe's markets. If the two dozen miles between Kent and Calais were as dry as the ink on the Rome Treaty, we should still be far from overcoming the heritage of our island past. For too many firms Europe is still uncharted territory, shrouded in mist and marked "here be dragons" as on the maps of the old explorers. And travellers' tales abound to buttress the stay-at-homes' fears of the unknown; the story of the roving European salesman who was sacked after failing to account for his time and expenses for three months, and was later discovered to be working "full-time" for two other British companies; the local distributor who ended up pirating the product under his own trade-mark; and of course the unfortunate and unintended double meaning in the sales literature translated by the Managing Director's secretary "who spoke perfect French". Much safer, perhaps, to stay at home.

But there are ways of bridging the gulf that all too often seems to yawn beyond the comfortable home market, and it does not require some totally new method hitherto unpractised at home. On the contrary, the use of unfamiliar practices in uncharted territory could increase the risks unnecessarily. This is certainly true of the first problem of all; whether to set up a European based salesforce, to rely on agents or distributors, or to sell into a European market from a UK base. Carrying out the research on which such a decision is based should not be too difficult for any firm that has done the same in its home markets; it may be a lengthier process and it may cost more, but (as Leslie Walsh shows in his article "How to research the EEC") it is not as daunting as is sometimes feared.

Distributor, agent or own sales force

The basic difference between the distributor and the agent is that the latter operates on a commission basis, while the former buys from the manufacturer and makes his profit on resale. In both cases the advantages are that they are on the spot, know the market and have the contacts. The agent has the attraction of being able to spread his costs over several accounts, he is paid by results and little investment is needed. These are important advantages when breaking into a market for the first time even though it may be intended at a later stage to set up your own sales force.

The disadvantage is that a commission basis offers no penalties for not selling, and many an agent can coast along happily on the commission from a few large orders or a wide spread of clients, with no real effort. The first requirement for a satisfactory agent is therefore that he should really want your business, but if he knows your long-term goal is a sales force of your own this could be a considerable disincentive. And do not forget that local laws often make it expensive to cast off agents.

But there are ways round both these problems. For instance. Dobroyd's Ltd., a Yorkshire woollen firm, restricts its German agents to the smaller outlets and deals direct with the largest garment-makers itself. This suits the big buyers who often prefer to buy direct and the agent can be kept happy by arranging for a reduced commission to be paid on business done in this way.

Distributors share with agents the advantage of being on the spot and knowing the market. There is the additional benefit that they also accept more of the commercial risk because they purchase and stock the product. This means also that they are providing some of the finance.

These advantages may often make distributors and agents the best way into new European markets, but the long-term drawbacks reinforce the case for regarding them as stepping stones to company controlled sales forces. An all-too-common mistake is to imagine that distributors and agents possess one advantage deliberately not listed above; that the whole marketing function can be handed over to them on the day the agreement is signed. In fact, an agent does not make it possible to avoid direct involvement because personal visits will still be necessary to provide technical help to customers, to help the agent with important negotiations and to chase the agent himself. Product training at the UK base will also often be a must for agents and distributors, and help with advertising and promotion is sure to be needed.

These costs may seem to reduce the attractiveness of indirect methods as a way in; if you are doing all this anyway why not sell direct? Why train agents' or distributors' staff when you could be training your own? But the agent/distributor set-up can nevertheless be a useful first step on the way to building up a company owned sales force. Agents can be put on a salary, and distributors can be bought up or bought into. Ideally this possibility should be built into the arrangement from the start. This is a technique that has been practised successfully by Queen's Award Winner Dexion-Camino International which has often made the takeover at a time when the business had outgrown the resources of the distributor. The company has also felt it necessary to take this step when a distributor has become unwilling to follow Dexion's policies. "Distributors", explains Group Marketing Manager Cyril Towner, "have a tendency to want to go their own way, which is not always in the best interests of the exporter".

Selling through visits from the UK

The nature of the product, the market and the distribution system must be taken into account before making decisions on the best way to sell. Where, as often happens in the industrial field, business is based on a comparatively small number of customers each placing large orders; where markets are geographically approachable, and in cases where products are tailor-made to each order, there are advantages to both buyer and seller in direct contacts. In particular, where the value of each contract is high, the cost of visits may well be less than an agent's commission, and the technical problems involved mean that the principal will have to be called in sooner or later anyway. Thus the Warwick firm of IHW Engineering Ltd. sells hinges directly into the German motor industry. Managing Director Harold Tomlinson calls personally on the small number of really large potential customers. And because German car makers call in the hinge manufacturer at the design stage, once a sale is made, the business is sure to last for several years ahead.

Direct selling by visits from the UK can also be the right way in the consumer field if a few large chains buying centrally represent the bulk of the market. But the drawbacks must be clearly faced; such customers will expect a visitor from the manufacturer's home base to be a fairly senior executive, and this may well prove too demanding on his time and energy. It does mean too that the executive making only occasional visits takes much longer to become truly familiar with the market – and this can cause mistakes.

Your own sales force

The first problem in recruitment is whether to employ continental or UK salesmen. The great advantage the European enjoys in terms of knowledge of the market and of local customs, language and attitudes, needs a lot of counterbalancing. In highly technical industrial markets, where expertise is central and technical knowledge transcends linguistic barriers, this may not matter so much (though a local with the right background would still score over a UK national). And some products, like Scotch Whisky or Yorkshire woollens, enjoy a certain cachet simply through being British, so a UK salesman could have an advantage. But in both cases, local salesmen can be employed if supplemented by visits from the UK. Motivation too must pose fewer problems with Europeans than with homesick UK salesmen who have suffered a traumatic upheaval of their social lives.

If the decision is to recruit Europeans, then there are four approaches which can be followed; advertising direct yourself; employing a consultant; using "unorthodox" methods of various kinds, such as head-hunting; and the indirect or "backdoor" approach.

The direct approach has a number of drawbacks for those approaching a new market from scratch. "Job markets are much tougher on the continent than they are here, especially compared with the present unemployment situation in the UK", says consultant Mike Wilson of Marketing Improvements Ltd., "and most UK firms would be shattered by the salaries and fringe benefits that would be expected". But although estimates of the salary differential go as high as 50 per cent above what is paid in the UK, this is counterbalanced by high salaries and expenses that would have to be paid to expatriate British reps. Such reps are likely to be tempted only by high salaries generous allowances for moving, for private English schools for their children, and or assistance in house purchase.

Selection agencies are thinner on the ground than in the UK, and job advertising is made harder by the absence of any real equivalent of the British national press, as well as by local laws that may attempt to prevent the "enticing" of employees from one job to another.

Some sales training organizations such as the Tack organization, have facilities for selecting salesmen through their subsidiaries in various European countries. So also do consultants such as Management Selection Ltd., which has subsidiaries or associates throughout the EEC. After detailed job specifications and man-specifications have been drawn up, MSL sees to the placing of job ads in the relevant European media. The company draws up the shortlist, on the basis of detailed enquiry into how the new appointee will fit into the client company's structure and who the persons are to whom and for whom he will be responsible. MSL can also advise on the form of the final contract, often an important point in view of the strong legal safeguards for salemen in continental countries. The fee for the whole service will in general be fixed at some 25 per cent of the first year's salary payable in instalments between the engaging of the consultant and making the appointment.

If you don't mind drawing up your own shortlist, and don't feel intimidated by the strangeness of the European market, you could dispense with a consultant's services; for a small firm, the expense of the fees may reinforce the case for going it alone. In this case you would need the services of an experienced recruitment ad agency such as Austin Knight, which has specialised for years in job recruitment advertising in Europe. Managing Director Kenneth Fordham finds he gets a better service through dealing direct with the media concerned, and not going through continental agencies as intermediaries. He might need more information from clients than a corresponding job in Britain would require, as the lack of national papers on the British pattern dictates a more finely tailored choice of media which will vary with the details of the appointment.

More unconventional is the "headhunting" method which is particularly suited to the selection of top executives, though John Reid of Executive Search Ltd. says that his firm would be happy to consider finding sales managers and the sales team as well as the sales executives. A firm champion of starting at the top is David Diehl of consultants Diehl Golightly and Co. SA. "The chances are you're in no position to choose staff in Europe", he says, "so first choose one key man who should probably be a European, and let him choose your European staff. Let it be someone who knows Europe and who is of such a status that you can respect his judgement and advice as you would that of your accountant."

The arguments in favour of "headhunting" as the way of finding such a key man are briefly that no one of the calibre you require is likely to be amongst the redundant or the insecure who, it is argued, are the only ones who read apoointment ads. But Sidney Simpson, European manager of MSL counters by pointing out: "We go out of our way to make our ads look attractive and people now look at management vacancy ads the way they look at the football results."

If that does not convince you, but you still feel put off by the headhunters' fees (which can also come to 25 per cent of the first year's salary or renumeration), you could try a bit of free-lance headhunting on your own behalf. One method recommended by Midlands consultant Ken Yarker is to start by identifying which of your successful competitors in the European market owe their success to a few key men. Then call each of them and explain that you are thinking of making an appointment yourself and "since you are in the same field as me, could you advise me?' You might find your man volunteering over the lunch that follows, if you mention the attractive terms and conditions.

Finally, there is the method we have already referred to, of clearly making one's relationship with an agent or distributor an intermediary stage to a closer tie-up. This could take the form of a takeover or joint company. Alternatively, a distributor's staff known to the UK company could be enticed away to form the kernel of its own force. But these solutions may not always be available, and are in any case no answer to a firm setting up from scratch.

Whatever method is chosen, the changeover to a sales force of one's own need not be a sudden switch. One example of the advantages of a gradual transition from agents to own salesforce is provided by Granada Publishing. Turnover doubled on appointment of a European Sales Manager who was able to see that priority was given to Granada's own products in the hardback field. But agents were still retained to help cover the large variety of specialist bookshop outlets; the European Sales Manager carries some lists himself, while other are carried by agents who work closely with him. "We see this," says Export Manager Ken Banerji, "as a half-way stage to giving the European Sales Manager an assistant who can take over 'in depth' coverage. This is an alternative to doing it all at once. We can let costs and sales rise together, and we are never budgeting too far ahead."

The training problem

Training is another problem which often intimidates those thinking of a sales force of their own. It can be broken down into company knowledge, product knowledge and selling skills. Training in the company's history, philosophy, and objectives is best done in the UK, and a home base may also be best for training in product knowledge; though beware of discussing product plusses and minusses in relation to the UK rather than the Continental competition. Though recruits will obviously have previous sales experience, further training may be necessary; this is best given in the country the salesman will be working in, as regional and national market variations may make the standard UK course a waste of time. Many UK sales training organizations too, will not have the necessary detailed knowledge of the European situation. On the other hand, if European sales training organization is used, it may be necessary to bring its staff over to the UK for product knowledge training.

British sales training organizations with an international spread, such as the TACK organization, will be able to offer in-plant training in Europe based on local experience. So can many international consultants, including the Institute's subsidiary, Marketing Training Limited. MTL offers training in Europe up to top management level, both for European salesmen in need of further training and for British sales personnel who need training in local conditions.

Another aspect of training which may pose problems is the language question. Here a variety of short training courses specially designed and tailored for business needs is available. The Business Services Division of Linguaphone, for example, offers a course based on colloquial language but with a special bias to the business environment and with vocabularies tailored to a firm's particular needs. The course is designed to equip the student for the intermediate level of the London Chamber of Commerce Oral Examinations. Incidentally, these oral exams also provide a useful means of checking the linguistic claims of job applicants.

Control and motivation problems

A salesforce of one's own offers greater potential for effective control and supervision than reliance on agents and distributors, but making that control effective remains a problem. The difference in market conditions can make it harder for management methods developed and proven in the UK to be simply transplanted.

The key to control is to develop a set of indices of performance based on long-term and annual plans. Performance can then be monitored by three- or four-monthly reports of profit and loss and turnover measured against targets set. Simplicity in this field is relevant to motivation also, and can make it easier to relate sales force objectives and salesmen's targets to company objectives. "The most successful sales forces," says Hedley Thomas, Director of Urwick Orr and Partners (UK) Ltd., "are those whose salesmen understand what the company is trying to do, and their part in it."

These problems, again, need not be different from those confronted at home. Regional and national market differences may mean, however, that pricing policy and promotion may have to be decentralized, in which case a system for central checking and control would have to be developed in these fields too.

Other aspects of sales force control also will not differ in essentials from the form they take at home, especially the need for adequate field supervision. This will necessitate an adequate ratio of field sales executives on the spot; this could cause problems with a force of fewer than six or so, and therefore reinforces the points made earlier in support of a gradual approach.

An interesting departure in financial control of a sales subsidiary is used by Ferranti Scotland for its German sales subsidiary, Ferranti-Intek. It finances itself from a standard commission on business done in its area. In this sense it is treated like a sales and service agency, with the difference that any profit after paying running costs subsequently reverts to the parent company.

Support

A sales force can be autonomous without being ignored. Salesmen are less likely to feel isolated and neglected if they are visited periodically by executives and specialists. Bill Stanley, TACK'S Managing Director stresses that executive visits are welcome to customers as well, who like to see the "big men" from the supplying company taking a personal interest in their custom. And technical visits from specialists give the salesman on the spot a useful back-up, especially where, as in most European countries, salesmen are not held in high regard by those with whom they have to negotiate.

Promotional support, however, need not be done from London. A large UK agency should have a European associate who can advise on laws dealing with questions such as premiums, or whether competitions are legally classed as lotteries. Fork-lift truck manufacturer Lancer Boss has a standard publicity manual available in English, French and German. With it, the company provides press releases on each truck, and blocks are available as illustrations, to assist in obtaining local coverage. Pictorially presented sales manuals and brochures with a minimum of text are also produced. This centralized approach may fit Lancer's product, but at the consumer end of the market cultural differences may dictate variations not only in the copy, but even in the illustrations, if they show the product in use. Differences in cuts of meat, or methods of laying the table, for example, can make domestic scenes look odd in foreign markets.

Nor do the arguments for technical visits relate only to the effect on the salesman and his activity. If home-based design, and research and development personnel can spend some time gaining first-hand contact with the customers alongside the salesmen, future product development can benefit. Similarly, regular Europe-wide meetings, especially when new products are launched, help to ensure a feedback of information on the state of the market, and make it possible for new product design to take account of different responses in the many different markets.

Conclusion

If the possible alternatives seem secondbest to a local sales force of one's own, the other methods of doing business can still be invaluable as a way round the obstacle of recruitment. And a variety of distribution methods may well be necessary to match national variations in distribution structure. Sales operations must often remain as obstinately national as distribution structures and consumer preference patterns. Thus one major firm of tractor manufacturers finds its product distributed in Finland by a farmer's co-operative, which sells through its local societies. In Norway it sells through a distributor who operates as wholesaler and retailer, while in Holland a wholesaler sells through a chain of independent retailers. In Germany, Italy and France the firm has its own factories which sell direct, a sales subsidiary in Eire does its own retailing, while the manufacturer sells through wholesalers in the home market.

Different methods of selling may well be required in different markets, especially in the earlier stages, and the methods employed may change over time. Continual checking is needed to ensure that the existing method for any market is still the optimum. But only when a local sales force is used instead of agents and distributors can it truly be said that overseas markets are no longer in a "different" category from home sales.

FINDING THE RIGHT SITE

Although good site selection is not enough on its own to give a guarantee of profit in retailing, it is difficult to be successful without it. Ralph Towsey of The National Cash Register Company explains a skill that is a mix of science and of old-fashioned "nose".

One would like to think that the title of this article implied that it is only necessary to look for a site that conforms to certain specified principles to be set for a nice profitable venture. If this were really so there would be far fewer planning mistakes and business failures. Unfortunately the finding of the right site rests not with the trader but usually with a very unpredictable planning authority, whose principles of consent often seem quite capricious. Hence the need for the recent recommendations by the NEDC and the Department of the Environment to planning authorities.

The right site, then, can usually be chosen only from a limited number which the planners will allow, but there are certain logical principles which should be applied when making the choice. In fact, it can be wiser to reject sites completely rather than take an economically unsound one merely because it is acceptable to the planners.

What is site assessment?

Before considering the principles governing the choice of site, site assessment (or site evaluation as it is sometimes called) must be put into perspective. It is not a complete determination of the viability of a retail project. In fact, it is not a *decisive* report in itself; it is a statement of facts about the site and its environment which must be interpreted in conjunction with other factors, such as those relating to return on investment, trading policy and company character.

There are schools of thought that range from the highly scientific, which believe that an assembly of facts can be brought together into a formula which can provide the ideal specification, to those which can be called the instinctive school – and having a "nose" for a site has proved very successful on a number of occasions. In practice, site assessment is a blend of both. It could indeed be ideal to be able to work to a specific formula, but it is quite impossible to quantify those subjective factors which attract a customer to one location rather than to others. Indeed, the customer herself may not even be able to identify those decisive elements. In practice, then, site assessment is based on the fundamental quesion: how can customers be expected to behave in given circumstances?

The objective

As with all successful management projects, the objective must be clearly defined. The objective of site assessment is to provide information which will help to determine whether a site is economically viable while conforming to the marketing objectives of the company. There are two implications here:

1. That an economic standard of operation must be set. This means the determination of a sales target which will not only provide enough profit to cover operating costs (which, too, must be calculated), but also yield a satisfactory return on the capital invested – a reasonable aim should be 20 per cent per year. At least this part of the exercise can be reduced to a specific formula.

2. The marketing objective must be clearly defined.

Marketing policy

This latter point is so fundamental that it deserves special consideration. If the main objective of a business is to increase its earning capacity, marketing policy is the method by which it is achieved. It must be definite, but at the same time sufficiently flexible to allow for changing demands, new marketing opportunities and, not least of all, locational policy.

We must start by establishing the marketing *purpose* of the proposed shop; is it:

(*a*) *To introduce the company to a new area? In this case we must ask ourselves whether the company's existing policy is consistent with the character of the neighbourhood in question, or if it is intended to adapt the shop's character accordingly. Some companies such as Woolworth, Marks and Spencer, Boots, W. H. Smith, and Sainsbury, have acquired a strong enough reputation to fit into any area. But even these companies succeed only because they are marketing for certain needs of all consumers, rather than for the needs of specific consumers. Furthermore, they usually have to adapt their detailed merchandising policies to the area in which they are situated.*

(*b*) *To remove from a declining to a developing area? This policy is so obviously sound as to need no comment.*

(*c*) *To provide convenience shopping for a neighbourhood, or to introduce specialized products where previously there had been none? This important question will be discussed in detail later.*

(*d*) *To take larger premises where existing ones have reached capacity? However, capacity should never be underestimated, a great deal can be done with interior replanning. Nevertheless, the tendency of most efficient retailers is towards larger shops which are more economical to run.*

(*e*) *To expand the scope for greater diversification?*

(*f*) *Or perhaps simply to enter the retail field for the first time?*

These last two points may imply a lack of knowledge, which could be restrictive. But one should bear in mind such modern techniques as franchising, concessioning, or simply "buying" knowledge, either by acquiring skilled people or just plain self-education.

Nature of consumer demand

One of the first decisions affecting locational policy, mentioned in (*c*) above, is whether the business is of a predominantly convenience or durable nature, because customer attitudes to each vary considerably.

The distinction is not always clear; but briefly, convenience goods are those which need to be replaced frequently and hence their purchase is less satisfying: food, tobacco, household preparations, medicinal and some toiletry products fall into this category. At the other end of the scale are such things as furnishings, radio and television, household appliances which are bought very infrequently and give much longer satisfaction. The intermediate ranges such as clothing, hardware, stationery, can fall into either category, but the deciding factor is the degree of satisfaction the purchase provides.

Location policy

The next decision to be taken is the sort of position in which the shop is to be:

(a) *The High Street offers high customer concentration, but suffers from high rents, parking restrictions and probably difficult access.*

(b) *Off High Street is less costly and parking may be easier, but customer flow is probably less.*

(c) *Precincts are designed for easy customer flow and attractive selection of shops, but are they easily accessible?*

(d) *Suburban sites are more economical, but may lack an attractive selection of shops. It is possible that rational planning policies in the future may mean a greater trend in this direction.*

Let us, then, consider the factors that will influence this choice:

1. Is the trade convenience or durable? From what has been said previously, we may assume that attraction varies *inversely* with the frequency of purchase, and customers tend to shop nearer home for convenience good. The point is illustrated quite clearly by the following table which is based on a supplementary report to the Census of Distribution 1961.

Proportion of trade in main shopping centres

Town size (*population*)	Convenience trades %	Durable trades %
200,000 plus	12	83
100,000 to 200,000	21	70
50,000 to 100,000	30	74
Less than 50,000	39	77

In this table, convenience trades are: food, confectionery, tobacco and newspapers. Durable trades are: clothing, household durables, other non-food shops.

(Note: The figures do not add up exactly to 100 per cent because median figures have been used, but the differences are insignificant.)

Two facts emerge quite clearly from the table:

(*a*) *The attitudes towards convenience and durable shopping are clearly distinguishable.*

(*b*) *The larger the town the less attractive is the centre for convenience shopping.*

2. Projected planning developments, for example, new or extended housing estates, new shopping developments which can shift the main focus of shopping. The study of planning developments cannot be too highly emphasized, and it may not be generally known that the information is accessible to anyone by reference to the local planning office.

Pedestrians need

Safe access, with particular regard to roads with heavy traffic – take note of the position of pedestrian crossings.

As little carrying as possible, hence the short distance customers will travel for convenience goods.

Freedom of movement, hence the preference for traffic-free precincts.

Public transport users need

Proximity of bus stations or bus stops. To avoid crossing main roads, whereever possible.

Bus shelters in case of bad weather.

Proximity of railway stations, where this is an important means of transport for the locality. In Stockholm, Rotterdam and Paris, shopping centres are actually located at suburban line stations.

Car shoppers need

As little congestion on roads as possible.

One-way systems which allow easy access and are not confusing.

Convenient and safe car parking. Even a small fee is acceptable if parking is satisfactory.

3. Relationship to other shops. A selection of shops has a much wider appeal than isolated ones, unless they are large enough to provide an attractive range in themselves. A fact which many retailers do not appear to realize is that competitive shops create an attraction by providing a wider choice. If the retailers in such places as Eastleigh would realize that a store like Carrefour would be a great advantage to them because it would widen the area of influence of shopping facilities, they might be less critical of it.

4. Observation of customer habits, which will be discussed in more detail later in this article.

The site itself

Having decided that the marketing policy is consistent with a site that is in a position conforming to the objective, let us test it in more detail.

The first point to look for is ease of access, taking into account those factors which customers need whether coming on foot, by public transport or by car. Incidentally, bear in mind that in the last 10 years the number of people who shop by car has practically doubled to a figure of about 30 per cent. and this figure will no doubt continue growing

Definition of catchment area

Of course no site is acceptable if it cannot draw on enough customers to provide the required turnover, and the definition of the catchment area – the area from which customers can reasonably be expected to come – is not only fundamental, but is unfortunately the most difficult element in the whole process of assessment.

This is the factor which assessors would dearly like to reduce to a scientific formula, and indeed many attempts have been made to do so. But of the three elements which influence it – proximity of customer to site, the site's inherent attraction of quality and services, and its relationship to other shopping facilities – the last two are to a greater or lesser extent subjective and difficult to use as elements in a formula. The definition of the catchment area, then, must be somewhat arbitrary, but should include as many objective elements as possible.

Of the methods available, I will mention three as being the most practical in my experience.

1. Index of shopping effectiveness

This term may sound rather ponderous, but it is given to a very interesting theory propounded by Professor Lichfield. Its basis is the quantitative relationship of the average amount of spending power in any given region to the actual spending in any centre in that region. The following example will explain the theory:

Average sales per person per year:

		Index
Hampshire county	£170	100
City of Winchester	£268	152
City of Southampton	£223	131

The inference is that the total amount of retail spending in Winchester is 52 per cent higher than the average for the county, therefore the catchment area for the city is its own population plus 52 per cent. The great advantage of this method is that it reflects customers' *actual* habits and we do not have to apply any of their opinions as to quality of shopping, ease of accessibility, and so on. A very interesting revelation is that Winchester appears relatively more popular than Southampton, despite the fact that the latter has a considerably wider selection of shops to choose from.

This same principle can be taken a stage further to assess the shopping effectiveness of individual trades, as shown in the following example.

Shopping Index

(Hampshire County – 100)

	Winchester	Southampton
Food	113	104
Confectionery, tobacco	106	106
Hardware	81	109
Chemists' goods	215	123
Clothing	202	147
Household durables	169	108
Misc. non-foods	225	98
Department and variety stores	228	224

Once again, we see the significance of the convenience/durable distinction. Furthermore, lack of popularity for convenience shopping in larger towns is borne out in the case of Southampton.

Probably one of the reasons why this method is not yet used extensively is that facts are rather out of date. However, I feel the method is so sound that it is worth investigating methods of extracting the information by private survey, though the 1971 Census of Distribution will supply valuable information provided that it is published within a reasonable time of its being taken.

2. Customer survey

This involves the simple interviewing of a proportion of customers frequenting the area surrounding the site to find out where they have travelled from. It is therefore factual and, provided a reasonable sample is taken, is probably the most accurate. R. K. Cox in *Retail Site Assessment* suggests 10 per cent as a good sample, but in practice NCR's site assessments have produced some remarkably accurate results with a 2 per cent sample. The only drawback to this method is the cost of time and labour in interviewing. Nevertheless, the interview can be used to ascertain other significant factors such as customer attitudes towards existing shopping facilities and how they can be improved.

3. The "observation" method

This is so named for want of a better term. It involves study of a map and of the actual area itself by an experienced assessor, who will base his observations on the three basic principles: proximity, attraction and relationship to other shopping facilities. He will first study a map of the area: a large scale map of about 6 inches to 1 mile for a convenience goods shop, and a smaller scale map for durables; for this purpose the 10 miles to 1 inch Ordnance Survey map showing local government boundaries is most suitable.

The assessor works on the principle that the preferred limit of walking distance to a shop is about 10 minutes, equivalent to about three-quarters of a mile. However, the arrangement of streets makes it impractical merely to draw a circle of 4 inches radius (on a 6 inches to 1 mile map). Furthermore, the assessor also knows that there are psychological and physical barriers to customer attraction. For example, customers will hesitate to cross a main road or railway or river and so it constitutes a boundary to the catchment area. It is from such factors as these that the assessor draws up his catchment area.

Not only will the assessor look at the area to determine the economic character of its population, but he will also use his experience to get other impressions. Among other things, he will observe:

(a) *The location and quality of competitors.*

(b) *The general trading atmosphere – whether it is thriving or declining. Evidence will be the appearance of other shops, and whether there are empty premises.*

(c) *Housing or shop developments which may shift the focus of shopping from one area to another.*

(d) *Apart from the economic character of the population, its age, size of family, ages of children, type of housing, proportion of houses with gardens, car population and, a factor which is often overlooked, ethnic groups (Jewish, Indian, etc.).*

Having defined the catchment area, the next step is to translate a geographic area into population terms. In practice, an assessor generally uses the medium of the household unit because the most useful document for estimating purchasing power is the

Family Expenditure Survey, published annually by the Department of Employment and Productivity.

To assist in determining the population of a given area, the assessor will try to ensure that local government boundaries coincide with his catchment area boundary. Population figures for such areas are readily available from local government records, or from the National Census; they are quoted in numbers of households as well as individuals.

The *Family Expenditure Survey* gives a comprehensive breakdown of weekly expenditure of a very broad analysis of goods and services, so it is easy to extract from it those commodities handled by the shop under assessment. It also analyses expenditure according to the economic class of the family. Therefore a careful personal examination of the area is necessary to try to put it into the right category according to the predominant character of the neighbourhood. Census records can also help here, because they break down the population into professional and occupational categories. If there is any doubt as to the economic classification of the area, I have found that one cannot go far wrong by using the overall averages from the *Family Expenditure Survey*.

These sources will enable a close estimate to be made of the total purchasing power of the commodity groups with which we are concerned. The next logical step is to examine the competition with which this purchasing power is to be shared. Mention has already been made of the assessor's observation of competitors, but he must now try to estimate how much of the available purchasing power they are getting. Means of estimating a shop's turnover are severely limited. The two most commonly used in practice are:

(*a*) *Relating sales area to a known sales conversion formula of sales per square foot. In this connection my only source of information is a confidential one, except in the case of food shops which have various published sources.*

(*b*) *Number of check-outs in food shops is also a very useful guide.*

Another method that is receiving careful study in professional circles is the relationship between rateable value of the premises (a figure easily available from the Local Rating Office) and turn-over. This method was discovered by G. W. Blackall when at National Cash Register Co. Ltd. He has done much research and has given several papers to professional planners and local government bodies on the theory. He has found that in most parts of the country the rateable value of grocers' shops is about 1 per cent of annual turnover, thus weekly turnover can be estimated simply by doubling the rateable value. In the case of other shops the percentage is about 1·7 or 1·8 per cent.

In practice, no one method of estimating turnover is used exclusively, and as many as possible are used for verification.

Conclusions

To sum up the main points:

1. Site assessment will not in itself determine the viability of a project.
2. It must be studied within the context of a clearly defined marketing policy.
3. It must be clearly established whether the business is predominantly of a convenience or durable nature.
4. The essence is the definition of the catchment area, which cannot be done absolutely scientifically because of the subjective elements in customer attitudes.
5. Customer habits are never static, they change with personal prosperity, economic conditions and planning developments, among other things.
6. Constant watch should be kept on planning developments. Information is readily available from the Local Planning Office.
7. A favourable assessment is useless unless followed up by good merchandising.

22

MAKING THE MARKETING PLAN

Planning in marketing is "a good thing", most would agree, but it tends to be one of those things "we are going to do next year". Perhaps it sounds too difficult. Joseph O'Hanlon of the American Sears, Roebuck, sets out in a simple form the essential framework for its introduction.

As business moves into the seventies and eighties it becomes increasingly obvious that there is a growing need on the part of management for a thorough, logical and systematic assessment of various factors involved in the marketing environment, including a current evaluation of consumer wants and desires, before commitment to a course of action. This basic idea was very well expressed by Theodore Levitt in his article *Marketing Myopia* where he said, "If you do not know where you are going, all roads lead there."

A marketing plan provides a disciplined approach to solving corporate and/or product marketing problems by ensuring that all aspects of the problems are considered in a systematic fashion. The written plan provides a means of achieving basic agreement, prior to any commitments, as to what constitutes the problem. It then forces an evaluation of the various means to overcome it. It guides management in making long range plans, and obviates the likelihood of costly improvising and changing of direction. It provides a time-proven method for achieving continuity of effort and direction that is vital for the successful accomplishment of a company's or product's objectives.

What is a marketing plan?

A marketing plan can be defined as a written document which:

1. Examines the major facts in the marketing situation under consideration.
2. Identifies the problems and opportunities inherent in the particular marketing situation.
3. Establishes specific long and short range corporate objectives for the product.
4. Proposes a long range strategy to solve the problems and to capitalize on the opportunities.
5. Recommends specific selling, advertising and promotional tactics to carry out short-range strategy and accomplish the objectives set for the next 12-month period.

The cost of planning is insignificant in comparison with the millions spent on advertising and promotion. It is well to remember that the best salesmen, the best creative staff and best media programme in the world will not match competitors who have superior selling ideas and programmes.

Advantages of a marketing plan

The advantages of a marketing plan were well summed up by Clarence Eldridge, an early pioneer in marketing plans, during the period he was executive vice president in charge of marketing for the Campbell Soup Company. He cited five reasons why he considered them necessary and desirable, namely:

1. Such a plan brings up to date the facts upon which the marketing strategy is based.
2. It assembles in one place all facts and thinking and to that extent becomes a self-contained and completely documented charter.
3. There is always a turnover in personnel on a product; the plan makes available to all the information necessary on the status and problems of the product.
4. It provides a desirable challenge to every element of the

promotional strategy i.e. expenditure, allocation, media, copy policy. Every element must be justified. It minimizes the possibility of continuing a strategy merely because nothing better has been suggested.

5. It helps to integrate all elements of the marketing mix – personal selling, advertising, promotions, etc. These elements are, or should be, considered in relationship to each other; they are all parts of the grand strategy and no one of them can be evaluated intelligently without a consideration of the others. Just as a media recommendation, in an advertising plan, cannot be intelligently arrived at without a thorough understanding of all the other parts of the advertising plan, so advertising strategy – as a part of the total promotional strategy – cannot be intelligently determined without a knowledge of the other promotional elements. The various pieces in the promotional pattern must be put together if they are to make sense.

Contents of a marketing plan

A typical marketing plan is most often divided into five main sections; namely:

Section I – Situation: This section enumerates all the major facts about the market, the consumer, competition, industry practices and your own product.

Section II – Problems and opportunities. Here you summarize the most important findings brought out in the situation and pinpoint them as either problems which need to be overcome, or opportunities on which you can capitalize.

Section III – Company objectives: In this section you should detail as far as possible what you wish to attain with regard to dollar/unit volume, market penetration, profits, etc., within the next five to ten years.

Section IV – Strategy (long range): This section spells out in broad strokes how you plan to accomplish your long range objectives: In this section you should cover, in a broad fashion, your long range planning with regard to sales volume, merchandising, pricing, copy, media, product changes, manufacturing, etc.

Section V – Tactics (short range): Here you spell out your specific objectives for the next 12 months and cover in detail exactly *how* you plan to accomplish them during the coming 12-month period. It should contain a schedule of who does what, to whom, when it is to occur and its estimated costs.

Section VI – Evaluation: Here you spell out the plans for evaluating the programmes you have covered in the Tactics section. While it may be considered optional in some marketing plans, it is always prudent to include it since it permits you to measure your performance in terms of accomplishing the objectives you have set for yourself.

Organization of the market plan

The following is a suggested outline of the information to be included in a marketing plan.

Section I – Situation

1. The size, scope and share of market

(*a*) Sales history of total market and market segments in units/£s (for, say, 5 to 10 years).

(*b*) Share of market by manufacturer's units/£s (5 to 10 years).

(*c*) Market potential and trend in supply and demand.

(*d*) Pricing history through all channels of distribution.

2. Sales, costs and gross profit of company product

(*a*) Sales history, by sizes or models, by sales districts.

(*b*) Cost history including cost of goods delivered, selling, advertising, administration, and all other expenses.

(*c*) Gross profit history (net before taxes) including competition (if known).

3. Distribution channels

(*a*) Identification of principal channels – sales history through each type.

(*b*) Buying habits and attitudes of principal channels, company product *vs.* competitors, including data on shelf frontage, inventory, turnover, profits and out-of-stock.

(*c*) Comparison of your selling practices and policies *vs.* those of your competition.

(*d*) Evaluation of your promotions relative to those of competitors, some measure of the relative effectiveness of each.

(*c*) Evaluation of trade advertising, literature and exhibits – your product *vs.* competition.

(*f*) Point of sales display material – you *vs.* competition.

4. *The consumer or end user*

(*a*) Identification of person making buying decision by demographic breakdowns.

(*b*) Consumer attitudes – your product *vs.* competition with regard to quality, price, packaging, styling, etc.

(*c*) Consumer purchasing habits – including place of purchase, cash or credit, frequency, etc.

(*d*) Consumer use habits – how, when, where, by whom, etc.

(*e*) Company advertising history – in terms of yearly expenditures, media, and copy strategy, results of advertising effectiveness tests and similar data on competitors.

(*f*) Publicity and other educational influences, strategy and effectiveness.

5. *The product*

(*a*) History of the product, quality development, design, sizes or models, packaging, labelling, delivery service.

(*b*) Comparison with competition – taste/use test results relative to competition.

(*c*) Product research, product improvement or changes planned.

Section II – *Problems and opportunities*

The "facts" developed in the Situation (Section I) constitute the basis for this section. Review the facts to determine specific problems or opportunities with regard to:

(*a*)   Total market
(*b*)   Market segments

(c) Trend development
(d) Competitive environment (share of market/penetration)
(e) Consumer:
   (i) Awareness
   (ii) Attitude
   (iii) Behavioural patterns
(f) Manufacturing costs
(g) Pricing
(h) Promotion
(i) Copy – creative strategy
(j) Media selection/strategy
(k) Consumer usage
(l) Profits

Section III – Company objectives

Objectives should be statements that clearly indicate *what* it is intended is going to happen when. Objectives should not be confused with methods. It is not an objective to say: "Increase consumer awareness in top markets through saturation TV." Rather, you should set as an objective for the next five years: "To increase overall consumer awareness of 'X' from the 5 per cent currently held, to 15 per cent in the top 50 markets, particularly among women, with secondary emphasis on men:

(a) Among the 25 to 35 age group.
(b) Among families with an income of £2,000 to £3,000 annually.
(c) Better educated – at least high school.
(d) Particularly those living in the west."

You should consider, depending on the situation, objectives covering the following areas:
(a) Sales
(b) Market share/penetration
(c) Promotion
(d) Pricing
(e) Distribution
(f) Advertising:

   (i) Copy
   (ii) Media
(*g*) Product design/quality/sizing
(*h*) Manufacturing/production
(*i*) Packaging
(*j*) Consumer acceptance/awareness/consumer research
(*k*) Competition
(*l*) Profits

Summing up, the key to writing objectives is to make them specific. Select a definite period of time for your intended progress. Use the company's goal to establish the overall outline of where you want to be at the end of a time period in terms of market franchise, volume and capital enhancement. Use your strategic objectives to describe the market conditions you hope to influence. In drafting objectives it is usually easier if you write general ones first, and them make them specific.

Section IV – Strategy (long range)

Strategy is essentially the specific plan or method you propose to use to accomplish your objectives over the next five-year or longer period. Once you have set the objectives, the next task is to cover the specific methods by which you plan to reach the objectives. Developing either long-range or short-range marketing methods requires ideas, imagination and creativity. The purpose of defining objectives first is to give guidance to your creative process of selecting a method which will accomplish your goal.

Generally, the process of planning can be reduced to three steps:

1. Define the objectives of the plan as simply as possible.
2. Get as many ideas as possible which might work.
3. Weigh each idea against the objective, and select the one which can best be developed to meet the objectives.

The Strategy Section consists of a broad outline of the steps you plan to take to accomplish each objective with regard to:

(*a*) Sales
(*b*) Share of market/penetration

(c) Promotion
(d) Pricing
(e) Advertising:
  (i) Copy
  (ii) Media
(f) Product/consumer research
(g) Product design/quality/sizing/research
(h) Manufacturing/production
(i) Packaging
(j) Consumer acceptance/awareness
(k) Competition
(l) Distribution
(m) Profits

Section V – Tactics (short range)

Since the Strategy Section covers a five-year period, the Tactics Section of the plan should cover only the coming 12-month period. Each of the tactical objectives covers a one-year segment of the five-year objectives spelled out in the previous section. The same applies to the actual plan itself. Here you spell out in detail who does what to whom, when, and the costs involved for the coming year. In the Tactics Section you map out immediate and specific advertising, promotion and sales objectives and then determine the best immediate and specific advertising, promotion and sales approaches to accomplish these objectives.

Here you spell out, for example:

Who the salesman is to call on; the story he is to tell; the promotional material, literature, etc., he needs to get his product sold; what the advertising is to say; how it will be said; when it will be said; and how to plan, co-ordinate and integrate all these efforts so that they augment each other and ensure that the entire marketing effort moves in the same direction at the same time.

Here you should consider in detail specific plans or programmes for the 12-month period with regard to the areas considered only broadly in the Strategy Section.

Section VI – Test marketing (optional)

While this section may be considered optional, it can be a very important and integral part of any plan. Test marketing provides a technique for measuring and evaluating the probable performance of the marketing tactics under actual marketing conditions. Evaluation is the essence of good planning. It ensures that the programmes are working and informs management of any unforeseen problems occurring in the market place which may necessitate a change in plans.

This section usually includes the following:

(*a*) Test market objectives
(*b*) Test market plan
(*c*) Test market selection
(*d*) Test market schedules
(*e*) Test market costs
(*f*) Responsibilities with regard to testing

Factors found in a good marketing plan

Now that we have discussed and defined the content of a marketing plan, let us examine the factors which are found in all good marketing plans.

All marketing plans should have certain ingredients in common. These are:

1. Specificity – the details of the plan must be specific enough for:

(*a*) Implementation
(*b*) Control
(*c*) Evaluation

2. Measurability – desired results have to be expressed in measurable quantitative terms.

3. Specific duration – this can be as long or as short a period as is thought reasonable to accomplish specific objectives.

4. Flexibility – provide for adjustment and change should evidence indicate that the initial programme is not performing as anticipated.

5. *Accountability* – the responsibility and authority for each phase of the plan must be clearly enumerated and communicated to all concerned.

How to use a marketing plan

Unless it is used properly, any marketing plan is merely a collection of papers and data and is completely lifeless until it is converted into action. It is therefore necessary to:

(*a*) *Treat the plan as an action document* – do not let it become an historical exercise.

(*b*) *Inform all concerned about the entire plan* – give a complete copy to every member of the company who is responsible for carrying out any portion of it.

(*c*) *Make someone in the company responsible* for seeing that it is carried out as written or to have approval of any and all deviations.

(*d*) *Review the plan regularly* – hold periodic reviews with all concerned to check the progress against the previously agreed upon goals. Issue a monthly report on progress.

(*e*) *Rewrite the plan as required* – a new marketing plan should be prepared whenever there is:

(i) A basic change in the product.
(ii) A basic change in the market.
(iii) Whenever the fiscal control period or marketing situation calls for a new plan. In any case, serious consideration should be given to a complete review and re-evaluation of the plan at least once each year.

Conclusion

Marketing plans represent a very modest cost relative to the magnitude of the results of successful marketing operations. The necessity for good planning increases as the difficulty of marketing increases. There are numerous indications that the present trend toward higher costs of doing business and greater competition in each marketing area will increase rather than diminish. The marketing executive who has the foresight to see where he wants to go, the ability to determine the best way to get there, and who takes the trouble to write it all down in a marketing plan, is very likely to achieve the success in the market place he is seeking.

And if, in spite of these arguments, you do not consider it worth while making a marketing plan, there is one important point you must accept. It is that in making such a decision you are saying either that changes in the marketing environment are unlikely to occur and to carry on as before is therefore satisfactory, or that changes may occur but you will be able to react to them quickly enough when they do occur. Either assumption is very dangerous.

It may be that it was possible to manage without a marketing plan in the past, but as the pace of technical development increases and as competition becomes more severe, it will become less and less possible.

23
A BOOK GUIDE
TO MARKETING

One expert's guide to the books the well-read marketing man should have on his bookshelf. Leslie Walsh, who is Director of International Marketing at PA Management Consultants, recently carried out a survey of the recommended reading lists of the UK universities and business schools to help in forming his opinion. So as well as giving his personal preference based on his wide reading, he gives us a "Top 25".

Marketing Director . . . the successful candidate will hold a university degree in marketing, preferably with majors in industrial and international marketing, as well as the Diploma of the Institute of Marketing. . . .

No, the advertisement has not appeared yet, but the day is perhaps nearer than we think when companies will demand from their marketing executives the formal qualifications they already require of their accountants and engineers. Certainly marketing education in the UK has made great strides in the few short years since the Institute of Marketing led the way to the first chair of marketing at a British university. Courses in marketing at universities and polytechnics, if they still do not exactly abound, at least present a wide choice. Marketing is becoming more professional every day.

But what of the present generation of company marketing executives? Are we to be swept away in the tide of professionalism, bellowing like dinosaurs about long-haired theorists or the value of a classical education, or shall we wish we "had 'em in uniform like in the old days"? No, the situation is hardly as desperate as that, and there are now available, in any case, some remarkably good textbooks with which the marketing executive can expand and up-date his knowledge. In fact, there are rather too many such books. These days the hard pressed executive has little enough time to spare from his main task of earning his own and his company's living. He can therefore read only a very limited number of books. Which should he choose?

Well, first of all, what are the UK universities and business schools recommending to their students? All those offering marketing courses were asked for a copy of their recommended reading lists, and a remarkably helpful response must be gratefully acknowledged. Often not merely reading lists were sent, but complete syllabuses and course programmes, with lengthy letters of clarification as well. If only industrial respondents were half as helpful!

In one sense the response was a little too helpful, for it soon became clear, if only because of the sheer variety in the nature and purpose of the courses, that a purely mechanistic selection of textbooks, on a head-counting, or rather recommendation-counting, basis was too facile an approach. Further, many of the reading lists referred inevitably to 1971 (they were requested before the start of the present academic year), so that a number of important recent textbooks could not be included. For these reasons, this article must remain to some extent one man's view.

Similarly, for reasons of space, it is possible to consider only general marketing textbooks and those covering certain major technique areas. This has meant, of course, that many first class works on narrower and more specialist areas have been ignored.

General marketing textbooks

It might seem a daunting, or even impossible, task to recommend which of the plethora of general marketing textbooks should take pride of place. Not a bit of it; the answer is obvious, and you probably know it already: it can only be *Marketing Management – Analysis, Planning and Control,* by Philip Kotler. With one or two specialist exceptions, it was recommended in every reading list received, often as a principal, or even *the* principal, course textbook. It was the only book to be so recommended so much.

Kotler starts right from first principles with the marketing concept and the marketing environment and covers every aspect of marketing in turn, from initial definition to the use of mathematical models. The book is a distillation of everything that is most up to date in marketing theory and practice – with the emphasis on that last word, practice. The author discusses more the *application* of marketing theory than the details of the theory itself, and never hesitates to indicate the limitations of theory in certain circumstances (as, for instance, in the field of pricing). Further, although he draws heavily on the behavioural sciences, economic theory and statistics, he makes almost no assumptions about the reader's prior knowledge. (For instance, if the phrase "mathematical model" puts you off, turn to page 227 of the first edition, where Kotler describes the same model verbally, diagrammatically and mathematically. At last it all makes sense.) In fact, for the first time we have available in one single volume the means by which the merest beginner can convert himself into a tolerably competent marketer. The second edition is now on sale, and there will be many more. Kotler will be as much a classic as *David Copperfield* or *Barchester Towers*.

But do not get the idea that it is particularly easy to read – even if it does not break new frontiers, there is some quite tough meat among its 600 pages. While it is essential reading for the marketing executive, it could prove a little too comprehensive for, say, the newly appointed managing director with an accounting or production background, anxious to take an early grip on his marketing function. What, for him, or for anyone else who is looking for a quick and simple introduction to the whole vast subject of marketing, is the best available textbook? Again there is a vast choice, and a very good chance that you end up with some turgid work that puts you off marketing for good. To avoid this fate, read the Macdonald and Evans handbook *Marketing* by G. B. Giles. Written in a terse, compact style, almost in note form, the book compresses modern marketing theory into 200 pocket-size pages. The most frequently recommended introductory work in the

Suggestions for the Top Twenty-five

Aspect of Marketing	Introductory Work	Standard Work
General	G. B. Giles *Marketing* Macdonald & Evans	P. Kotler *Marketing Management— Analysis, Planning and Control* Prentice Hall
Market research	A. H. R. Delens *Principles of Market Research* Crosby, Lockwood & Son	R. M. Worcester(ed) *Consumer Market Research Handbook* McGraw-Hill Book Co. A. Wilson *The Assessment of Industrial Markets* Hutchinson
Sales forecasting	A. Battersby *Sales Forecasting* Penguin Books	G. J. Bolt *Market and Sales Forecasting —A Total Approach* Kogan Page F. Keay *Marketing and Sales Forecasting* Pergamon Press G. Wills *et al.* *Technological Forecasting* Penguin Books
Product policy	D. W. Foster *Planning for Products and Markets* Longmans	T. L. Berg & A. Schuchman (eds.) *Product Strategy and Management* Holt, Rinehart & Winston
Distribution channels	N. A. H. Stacey & A. Wilson *The Changing Pattern of Distribution* Pergamon Press	B. E. Mallen (ed.) *The Marketing Channel – A Conceptual Viewpoint* John Wiley & Sons

Pricing strategy R. A. Lynn
Price Policies and Marketing Management
Richard D. Irwin

S. A. Tucker
Pricing for Higher Profit
McGraw-Hill Book Co.

Suggestions for the Top Twenty-five—*continued*

Aspect of Marketing	Introductory Work	Standard Work
Pricing strategy	B. Taylor & G. Wills (eds.) *Pricing Strategy* Staples Press	
Advertising and promotion	O. Ellefsen *Campaign Planning* Business Publications	R. H. Stansfield *Advertising Manager's Handbook* J. C. Aspley & O. Riso *Sales Promotion Handbook* Dartnell Corporation
Sales management	D. W. Smallbone *An Introduction to Sales Management* Staples Press	D. W. Smallbone *Control of the Field Sales Force* Staples Press
Management sciences in marketing	P. Kotler *Marketing Decision Making: A Model Building Approach* Holt, Rinehart & Winston	
Statistics for marketers	K. A. Yeomans *Statistics for the Social Scientist* I *Introducing Statistics* II *Applied Statistics* Penguin Books	
International marketing	E. O. Stanley *Handbook of International Marketing* McGraw-Hill Book Co.	or G. E. Miracle and G. S. Albaum *International Marketing Management* Richard D. Irwin

reading lists was *Marketing: An Introductory Text*, by M. J. Baker.

Market research

Of several useful introductions to market research, the best is probably that old favourite, *Principles of Market Research*, by Delens, which was first published as long ago as 1950, but still appears in the reading lists. If you have never been able to grasp the concept of the standard error, if you just don't know how those smart research chaps can assess the size of the sample in advance, if you have not the vaguest clue on significance testing, Delens is your answer. Not that statistics take an undue prominence in the book – the whole field of consumer research is covered, including at least a mention of some of the more specialized areas of the technique.

For the standard work on market research it would have been necessary, up to a few months ago, to refer to one of several American textbooks on the subject. But as most marketing executives will now know (McGraw-Hill's advance promotion being as efficient as ever) we now have available the *Consumer Market Research Handbook* (edited by R. M. Worcester). The book was reviewed fully in the September issue of *Marketing*, and there is no need for further comment, except to say that it meets an obvious need and will probably become the standard work in future. (It does not, of course, in view of its recent publication date, receive a mention in any of the reading lists.)

The above books specifically cover consumer research, although the industrial researcher will nevertheless find them of real value. The latter will also need, however, the *Assessment of Industrial Markets,* by Aubrey Wilson (not the earlier work *Industrial Marketing Research* by Stacey and Wilson, though this was still recommended in some reading lists).

Forecasting

Forecasting is not an area where the marketing executive is particularly well served in terms of textbooks. The usual introduction, recommended in several reading lists, is *Sales Forecasting* by A. Battersby. It will be of particular help to the marketer anxious to understand time series analysis, on which it largely concentrates.

The standard work is even more elusive. More advanced works on forecasting tend to involve themselves in forecasting the national economy, or certain industry sectors of it, or with advanced statistical reinforcements – none of which is of immediate concern to the company marketing executive. A combination of three books is recommended as a compromise solution.

The first, *Market and Sales Forecasting – A Total Approach*, by G. J. Bolt, covers not merely time-series analysis, but, in an effort to discourage what the author calls "naive extrapolation of historical sales data", discusses subjective, non-statistical methods as well, and puts forward an overall forecasting framework. Perhaps because it is so recent (it was published only last year) it does not appear in any of the reading lists received.

In his statistical approach, Bolt is not very much more detailed than Battersby's introductory work. For a broader treatment of statistical methods, but one still aimed at what the author calls "management application level", try *Marketing and Sales Forecasting*, by F. Keay. Although published only this year, Keay already has one or two recommendations in the reading lists.

Technological forecasting is a special aspect of the subject which Battersby does not mention, and to which Bolt can devote comparatively few pages. The industrial marketer, at least, will need to go further. There are several American textbooks, and, of course, the well-known OECD publication by Jantsch. The British marketing executive, however, will probably prefer the home-grown product *Technological Forecasting – The Art and its Managerial Implications* by Gordon Wills and others.

Product policy

Too many textbooks on product policy tend to concentrate on new products and diversification. They dismiss the wider concept of overall product strategy, and the problems of range rationalization, in comparatively few pages. Indeed, many limit themselves entirely to diversification. Others tend to start off on a broad basis and then concern themselves so much with the details of the new product launch that they degenerate imperceptibly into general marketing primers with a new-product slant. One very recent book – too recent to appear in more than the odd reading list – which manages to steer an avoiding course between these twin dangers is *Planning for Products and Markets* by D. W. Foster. At 300 and odd pages it is a little too hefty to describe as an introduction, but it is all good value.

These same dangers are perhaps more easily avoided in a book which is a collection of articles; each article can – indeed must, by definition – concentrate on a specialist aspect of product policy. This format for once, then, is a definite advantage in *Product Strategy* (edited by T. L. Berg and A. Schuchman). It is recommended in several reading lists. Inevitably, the book includes Levitt's classic article "Marketing Myopia".

Distribution

One American academic has gone on record as saying "The study of distribution channels, and why they take various forms, is one of the most neglected areas of marketing today." You can say that again, and not just about marketing academics, either. For many of us, distribution channels are fixed, the marketing equivalent of the legislative code of the Medes and the Persians. We know very well that changing established channels is one way, and a very good way, of stealing a march on our competitors: we also know it is a very good way of going broke, so we let well alone. When we enter a new market, we know that innovation in distribution can lead to quick success: we also know it can lead to even quicker failure, so we follow the leader. Just occasionally, some provocative fellow (probably one of those long-haired theorists) refuses to accept the conformist status quo and literally spoils the market. Then the channels change underneath us, the goods flow through other outlets, and we are left high and dry. At least we do not get our feet wet on the way to the Labour Exchange.

All this means that there are very few textbooks on distribution channels and that we ought to read very carefully those that there are. Perhaps first of all we should read a general description of distribution patterns and their development. None is better than *The Changing Pattern of Distribution*, by Stacey and Wilson (with several recommendations).

But after that we should be seeking the theory of distribution, the concepts and the tools that will help us to think our own way through our own particular problems, to evaluate – or even simply to recognize – the opportunities that arise. For this we need a book that prescribes rather than describes. In fact, we need

The Marketing Channel – A Conceptual Viewpoint (edited by B. E. Mallen). It is a collection of articles again, analytical rather than descriptive, theoretical and proud of it, and recommended in a number of reading lists. Read it, convert the principles into practice, and send your competitors dry-shod to the dole queue.

If you are one of those unfortunate marketers who are also responsible for physical distribution, you will not have missed the review of *Marketing Logistics and Distribution Planning* in the October issue of *Marketing*. "Unfortunate" is perhaps an unfortunate word, since the declared aim of the book is to tie physical distribution planning in with the total marketing plan. But do get your channels right in marketing terms before you start to drive your lorries along them.

Marketing is all about profits, and a crucial factor in profits is price. So you would naturally expect that pricing strategy would be a constant preoccupation of the marketing executive. We all know, regrettably, that it is not. In fact, after distribution channels, pricing strategy (as opposed to today's price levels) is one of the last things he thinks about. It is the same, just for once, in the US: Udell undertook a small survey and concluded that "Business management did not agree with the economic views of the importance of pricing – one half of the respondents did *not* select pricing as *one of the five important* policy areas in their firms' marketing success."

Of course, in certain markets, such as the organized commodity markets, price is dictated by external factors, and the individual company has little or no room for manoeuvre. Others have long ago given up price theory as the over-simplified domain of the impractical economist. In fact, it is only in the last 25 years that marketing academics have turned their attention seriously to the practical application of price theory.

All this means that literature on practical pricing policies is even more limited than that on distribution. There can be no question of selecting a simple introduction and one standard work. For pricing strategies (and the basic economic theory behind them) try Robert A. Lynn, *Price Policies and Marketing Management*. For an accounting-oriented approach (but one which will help you to beat the accountant at his own game) try *Pricing for Higher Profit*, by Spencer A. Tucker.

Neither of these two American books received more than the odd mention in the reading lists, but it would be as well to get them under your belt before you tackle a longer British work, well recommended in the reading lists, *Pricing Strategy* (edited by Bernard Taylor and Gordon Wills). The book is another collection of papers by leading authorities and, with the best part of 600 pages, a pretty formidable collection at that. But you will not need to read it all – not every article will be relevant to your problems – and it would be surprising if you did not find something in it that was not only of interest but of practical value in improving the profits of your company.

Advertising and promotion

There is no shortage of textbooks in this area – rather a bewildering array of titles on every conceivable aspect of the subject. The problem of selection is at first sight formidable, but it becomes less so if one looks for one single book, complete in itself, covering the whole vast subject, from the point of view of the company executive rather than the agency. On these criteria we come back to the Dartnell Corporation's *Advertising Manager's Handbook*, or, if your interests are essentially below the line, the *Sales Promotion Handbook*.

As their titles imply, these books are more works of reference than textbooks intended for academic study. It is perhaps for this reason that neither is recommended in the readings lists (although, curiously, only a very limited number of books on advertising and promotion received any sort of mention). It must be admitted, too, that Dartnell handbooks tend to go in for crisp, dogmatic statements rather than carefully argued conclusions; perhaps, even in 1,000 pages or so, there is not, on so vast a subject, room for very much else. And, although the handbooks are regularly revised and up-dated, the format and illustrations are oddly redolent of the 1930s – particularly unfortunate, perhaps, in books concerned with advertising and promotion. For all that, one of these books has stood the test of time through many editions and revisions and they will both see many more editions in the future.

The simple introduction? Again, there is a wide choice, but you could do a lot worse than that classic of the late fifties, *Campaign Planning*, by Olaf Ellefsen which is still valuable in the seventies.

Sales management

For an introduction to sales management, try the book of that name by D. W. Smallbone. For the standard work, the sales manager would probably prefer *Control of the Field Sales Force*, by the same author. The larger book includes a wealth of sample recruitment application forms, typical recruitment advertisements, and training programmes. This is no ivory-tower book – it is specifically aimed at making the sales manager's task easier, and the sales force more efficient and more successful.

Like other books on the subject, however, it tends to shy away from the vastly difficult, but fundamentally important, problem of territory potential. Smallbone briefly dismisses the question, telling us that the methods of assessment of potential vary with each company and product. True indeed, but a few suggestions as to how we might set about the task would not come amiss. Stanton and Buskirk, *Management of the Sales Force*, devotes a chapter to the subject and lays down at least the guiding principles. In this and other respects it is a more analytical work and perhaps for this reason tends to be the preferred textbook in the reading lists concerned with sales management.

Management sciences

"A good many marketing executives, in the deepest recesses of their psyches, are artists, not analysts. . . . They enjoy flying by the seats of their pants. . . ." If you are a seat-of-pants flyer, you will not be interested in Kotler's newer book *Marketing Decision Making: A Model Building Approach*. If, however, you are in the habit of asking yourself from time to time whether the judgement decision you are taking can be improved, whether the issue can be clarified or quantified with the aid of mathematics, then this is the book you have been looking for. Not that it is an easy book for the non-statistician – some knowledge of calculus and probability theory is assumed. On the other hand, it would be a mistake to underestimate its value even to the completely non-numerate marketer. Kotler's verbal arguments are detailed and clear, models are classified under distinct headings (such as "Distribution", "Price", "Sales Force", "Brand Share"), and it requires no more than a few minutes' reference to check whether models can help and, if so, exactly how.

Kotler's book is a recent publication (1971) and probably appeared too late to figure in many reading lists. The earlier work by Montgomery and Urban *Management Science in Marketing* was more frequently recommended. There are several other American books on the subject, only one or two of which received even a mention.

Statistics

The choice of statistical textbooks is infinite and to the statistician probably most of them are helpful and all of them are comprehensible. But what about the company marketing executive, who begins to feel the need for a deeper knowledge of statistical theory, and whose knowledge of mathematics ended with O-level algebra or before? He will perhaps have groped among the standard statistical works, will have moved with relief to books that cover business mathematics, and then fallen eagerly on those claiming to specialize in mathematics for marketers. In all cases, he will probably, like Omar Khayyam, have come out by the same door as in he went. What he really needs is a book which makes no assumption whatever about his mathematical ability, but starts from first principles, with careful verbal explanations. In 1968 Penguin books produced one: *Introducing Statistics – Statistics for the Social Scientist, Volume One* and *Applied Statistics – Statistics for the Social Scientist, Volume Two*, by K. A. Yeomans.

On the first page of volume one Yeomans starts us off by telling us that $+$ means add and $-$ means subtract. "Yes," you will say modestly, "actually I knew that already." But, still on the first page, are you quite so happy with $\backsimeq$, $\div$ or $\eqsim$? If not, then this book is the answer to your prayer. In a dozen pages you will have revised as far as logarithms, and, slightly surprised, you will find you actually understand the *principle* behind them, something that no one thought to explain to you at school. A chapter or two later, a diagram explains the principle of least squares, and for the first time simple regression really does seem simple. This, in fact, is the secret of Yeomans' success: he explains, in words or diagrams as well as in figures, the basic principle, *why* a thing should be so. The whole book is a classic of the art of logical exposition.

International marketing

Five international marketing textbooks (all American) received a mention in the reading lists, and, of these, *International Marketing Management*, by Miracle and Albaum, had a slight edge on the remainder. The international marketing executive would prefer either this book, or more probably, the immensely practical *Handbook of International Marketing*, by E. O. Stanley. The latter book is packed with practical advice, on almost a check-list basis, but, sadly, this is an area where an American orientation is a serious disadvantage – much of Stanley's work is irrelevant in a UK context. There are several short UK works on international marketing, but no definitive text.

Conclusion

So there it is, a selection of fewer than 30 books, introductions and standard works, in the hope that it will prove helpful to the company marketing executive. You disagree with the selection? Well, we'll not quarrel about that: "What's one man's poison, Signor, is another's meat and drink." What's that? You haven't time to read either these books or any others? This theory is all very well, but in the real business world marketing is all a matter of drive, judgement, experience and personality? Well, most people would go quite a long way with you on the importance of these qualities in marketing and in business generally. But if your views really are as categoric as they sound, perhaps it would be helpful to recommend one last book. It is quite short, only 63 pages, and it is called *Bluff Your Way in Marketing*.